State in Flutter

A Guide to State Management in Flutter

Sanjib Sinha

Table of Contents

How do you rebuild widgets in Flutter?

When Should I call setState Flutter?

3. What is callback in Flutter? How do you pass a function in Flutter?

What is callback?

What is callback in Flutter?

How do you call widgets in Flutter?

4. What is a map in Flutter? How do you map a list in Flutter?

What is the key concept of State Management in Flutter?

What is a map in Flutter?

How do you map a list in Flutter?

5. Why is state management in Flutter? What is flutter state?

How we change the widget state in Flutter?

How to manage state of child through parent widget?

How do you use stateful widget Flutter?

How a Child Widget exports its state to its parent

How Child Widget implements this special property?

How the export and import of state take place

6. How many types of widgets are there in Flutter?

What are visible widgets?

What are the widgets in Flutter?

How do I create a Custom widget in Flutter?

7. What is inherited widget in Flutter, how do you use state management?

What is InheritedWidget in Flutter?

How do you manage state efficiently?

InheritedWidget manages state efficiently, but is that all?

How do you use an inherited widget in Flutter?

We keep our inherited widgets in a separate folders

How do you manage state through inherited widgets?

Extending state management to the second uncle and his child

8. What is flutter provider? How does provider flutter work?

Why we need a Model?

9 . How do you use Provider Consumer to manage State in Flutter?

How do you use Provider Consumer?

What is the Problem in managing state in Flutter?

How Flutter helps us to manage State?

How could we notify Listeners?

The Specific Steps to use Consumer widget

10. How do you use onPressed in flutter?

How do you use onPressed in flutter?

How do you call a function in flutter?

What is flutter function?

What is callback in flutter?

1. Getting Started

Before getting started, let me tell you one thing. Always use the latest Provider package for state management. And always maintain the Null Safety.

I also strongly recommend to read the latest and updated articles on Flutter .

Download Latest Flutter

To start with, we need to download the Flutter framework.

That is our first task. We need to go to The installation page of Flutter page, from where we will download and install Flutter.

We will start with Windows, first.

By the way, before delving into the book, I'd like to tell you that I write regularly on Flutter and Dart programming language at ZeroDotOne. For more Flutter related Articles and Resources

Who should read this book?

This book is intended for Intermediate and Advanced learners, and professionals who although have learnd Flutter, but still want to know more about Flutter State management best practices.

I know some of them still struggle with the concepts of State management in Flutter, as there are too many options available.

In fact, when there are too many options are available, developers often find it difficult to pick up the right one.

I hope this book will not only guide them to find the right choice, but at the same time, it will help them understand how State object in Flutter works underhood.

As I have just said, there are too many options. With reference to that, I have added a note later. But let us see the options at one glance.

How many options are there in Flutter?

Let us explore that first. And after that, we will start our journey to understand Flutter state management best practices.

By the way, if you are an absoluter beginner who want to start learning Flutter along with Dart programming language, then please download my previous book ** Beginning Flutter with Dart **

Beginning Flutter with Dart

Many options to manage State in Flutter

```
 1  1. StatefulWidget
 2
 3  2. InheritedWidget
 4
 5  3. ChangeNotifier with Provider
 6
 7  4. ValueNotifier with Provider
 8
 9  5. StateNotifier with Provider
10
11  6. Riverpod
12
13  7. BLoC library
14
15  8. MobX
16
17  9. Redux
18
19  10. Fish Redux
20
21  11. Async Redux
22
23  12. RxDart View Model
24
25  13. StreamProvider
26
27  14. Flutter Hooks
28
29  15. And Many More...coming!
```

We must stick around one great choice, that is Riverpod state management library, and will learn how to use it in detail.

However, before understanding Riverpod I think it is mandatory to undertand the Provider package and its limitations.

At the end of the book, if you have any question, feel free to contact me at: **
sanjib12sinha@gmail.com **

Flutter for Windows

Clicking the download button will automatically start downloading ziped Flutter in
your Download folder.

It would be around 700 MB in size. While extracting the file it would take around
1.30 GB place of your hard drive.

You may copy that extracted file to elsewhere, or you may keep it there (figure 1.1).

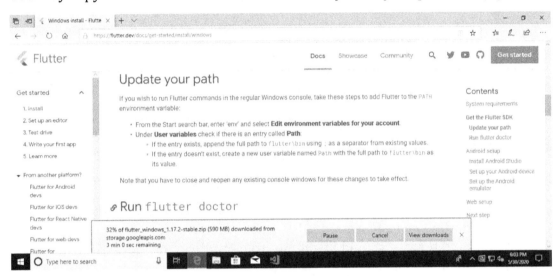

Figure 1.1 – Downloading Flutter for Windows

We have kept the extracted flutter folder there and created a new 'environment'
path for the user. Because we want to work through the command prompt, in future,
we have created this global environment path.

Creating a new environment variable path in any Windows operating system is also
easy.

In the Windows 10 operating system, we type 'environment variable' in the search
prompt, it will automatically open up the related window for us.

We can copy and paste the whole path there as the following:

```
1 "C:\Users\Downloads\flutter\bin".
```

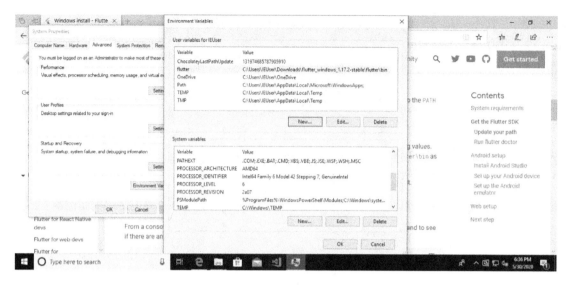

Figure 1.2 – Creating the new environment variable path in Windows 10

Now, we can open the command prompt and type 'flutter doctor' to see whether we have any Flutter related IDE installed already. It will also check whether we have any connected device or not.

We have not installed Android Studio or any other Flutter related IDE beforehand. The command 'flutter doctor' has detected that (Figure 1.3).

To work with Flutter, we need a good IDE. In fact, when we were downloading Flutter, it indicated that we should install Android Studio or any good IDE where we would have a connected device.

The connected device is nothing but a virtual mobile device where we can see and test our mobile application.

We need the Android Studio IDE first. It should be the best choice for one reason. You cannot create a virtual device without the help of Android Studio.

However, later I am going to use Visual Studio Code IDE. I have found VS Code more flexible in writing code.

It is widely used.

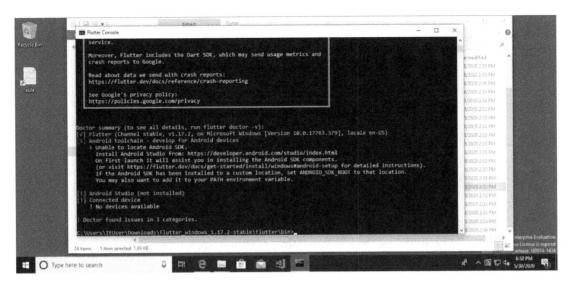

Figure 1.3 – Flutter Doctor Summary in Windows 10

In Flutter Doctor summary, we have found that Android Studio has not been installed and there is no device available.

Next, we will also learn how to install Flutter in our macOS and Linux machines. You can use any one of that operating system to learn Flutter and Dart together.

Flutter for macOS and Linux

Downloading Flutter for macOS and Linux is same. It will download the "flutter_linux_1.17.2-stable.tar.xz" file in your "Downloads" folder.

Next we will issue the following command to extract Flutter, on our terminal:

```
1 //code 1.1
2 tar xf flutter_linux_1.17.2-stable.tar.xz
```

Now we can copy this extracted 'flutter' directory to a suitable place, where we will build our first mobile application. In the 'Documents' directory, we have created another directory named 'development'. We will keep the extracted 'flutter' directory there.

Just like Windows 10, we will now set the global path for 'flutter', so that we can use 'flutter' command, anywhere in our machine, in the future.

We will do that using 'vim' or 'nano' text editor, that works on the terminal. By the way, the commands are same for any macOS or Linux operating system.

If you type the following command, the nano text editor will open up the 'bashrc' file.

```
1 //code 1.2
2 nano ~/.bashrc
```

At the end of the 'bashrc' file we will add this line:

```
1 //code 1.3
2
3 export PATH=$PATH:/home/ss/Documents/development/flutter/bin:$PATH
```

We have to mention the full path as given above. We have kept our extracted 'flutter/bin' folder in the '/home/ss/Documents/development' directory.

Our next step will be to download the Android Studio. Download the zipped folder and extract it anywhere in the machine. We have kept it in our '/home/' directory. Next, issue this command:

```
1 //code 1.4
2 ss@ss-desktop:~$ cd android-studio/bin/
3 ss@ss-desktop:~/android-studio/bin$ ./studio.sh
```

It will open up the Android Studio for us (figure 1.4).

Once the Android Studio opens up, you can go to the 'open folder' option and choose the flutter project we have created already. How we have created it, we will come to that point in a minute.

Before that, we need to see the Android Studio and our newly created virtual device.

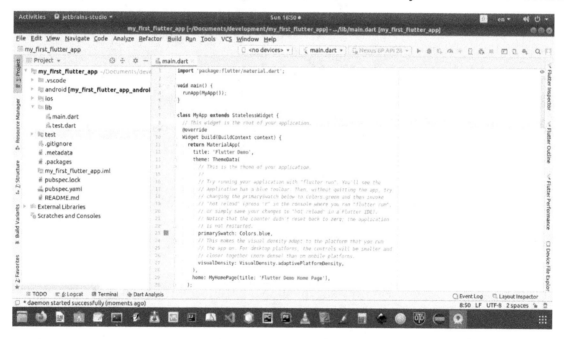

Figure 1.4 – Android Studio and our first flutter project

Before opening the Android Studio, we have opened up our terminal, and typed the following commands to reach to the newly installed 'flutter' directory.

```
1 //code 1.5
2 ss@ss-desktop:~$ cd Documents/development/flutter/
3 ss@ss-desktop:~/Documents/development/flutter$ flutter doctor
4 Doctor summary (to see all details, run flutter doctor -v):
```

```
 5 [✓] Flutter (Channel stable, v1.17.2, on Linux, locale en_IN)
 6
 7 [✓] Android toolchain - develop for Android devices (Android SDK
version 29.0.3)
 8 [✓] Android Studio (version 3.5)
 9 [✓] Android Studio (version 4.0)
10 [✓] IntelliJ IDEA Community Edition (version 2019.3)
11 [✓] VS Code (version 1.43.2)
12 [!] Connected device
13     ! No devices available
14
15 ! Doctor found issues in 1 category.
16 ss@ss-desktop:~/Documents/development/flutter$
```

As you have seen in the above output, 'flutter doctor' has found only one issue. It has not found any connected device. Otherwise, we have already installed Android Studio (version 4.0), which is the latest at the time of writing this book. We have also installed IntelliJ IDEA Community Edition, and we have also Visual Studio Code IDE.

We can use the virtual device from Android Studio, but we can use the Visual Studio Code IDE or IntelliJ IDEA Community Edition IDE for writing our code.

They will automatically synchronize with the connected device.

However, before that we need to create our first flutter project with the help of flutter command as the following:

```
1 //code 1.6
2 flutter create my_first_flutter_app
```

We must remember one thing.

When we want to create a new flutter project, we should always create like the way I have just shown above. The naming convention is important here.

We can only use the underscore between the words. No hyphen or space is allowed.

Now the time has come to go back to the Android Studio. We will pick up the 'open folder' option and choose to open the newly created flutter project. We have named it as: 'my_first_flutter_app'.

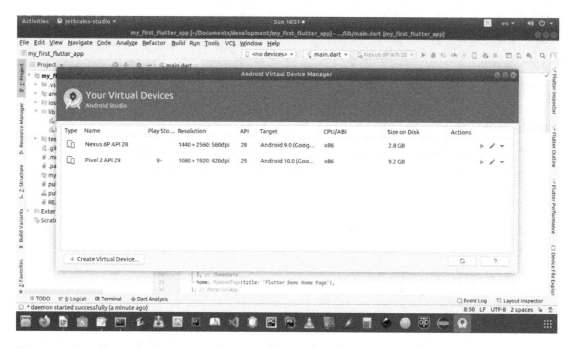

Figure 1.5 – Open the Android Virtual Device (AVD) manager from tools menu

To open up the connected device, we need to open the Android Virtual Device manager, or AVD manager in short.

You will get that from the 'tools' menu.

Select any one of them and click the 'green' play button on the far right hand side of any virtual device. It will automatically open up the 'connected device' (Figure 1.6).

Figure 1.6 – We have the connected device on which we can test our first mobile application

Now everything is ready. We can start building our first mobile application from scratch using Flutter and Dart. Before closing down this section, we should know a few good tips. Usually, the beginners encounter a few errors when they try to run the command:

```
1 flutter doctor
```

If it gives any error, try this command:

```
1 flutter doctor --android-licenses
```

It will ask you to accept the license. Accept it, and it will not give any error anymore. Another problem often gives trouble to the new developers.

As a beginning Flutter developer, people often are stuck with this issue.

They cannot launch the virtual mobile device while working with Android Studio.

We want that every code we write should reflect on the virtual device. It can be done by going to the 'AVD manager' from tools. But sometimes an ugly error pops up its head and tells that '/dev/kvm permission denied'.

In Ubuntu 18 or Mac OS, you can give user the permission by issuing this command:

```
1 //code 1.7
2 sudo chmod 777 -R /dev/kvm
```

But it has a drawback. If someone else uses your machine, then the other user also gets the permission.

The best remedy is – give permission to yourself only by the following commands:

```
1 //code 1.8
2 sudo apt install qemu-kvm
3 sudo adduser your-username kvm
4 sudo chown your-username /dev/kvm
```

It will solve the issue for ever. Now you can launch any virtual device you want. You can launch the device with your Android Studio, and work with any other IDE like IntelliJ or Visual Studio.

For more Flutter related Articles and Resources

2. What is the difference between stateless widget and stateful widget in Flutter?

We can create either stateless widget, or stateful widget. Strictly speaking, when a widget interacts with users, it's stateful.

And the opposite is also true. A stateless widget never changes.

However, the concept of state in Flutter is not that easy and simple as it appears in the above statement.

Why?

In this introductory Chapter 2, we will try to understand that.

The stateful widget has an internal state that is absent in the stateless widget.

As we see in both cases the UI gets re-rendered when input data changes. However, in stateful widget the UI also gets re-rendered when the internal state or local data changes.

The following diagram will help you to understand the core concept of state management in Flutter. However, I'll explain it later.

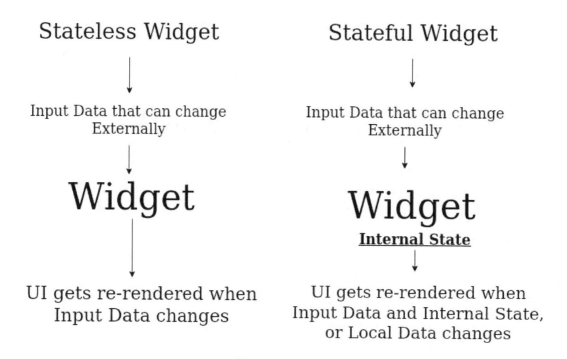

Figure 2.1 – What is the main difference between Stateless and Stateful Widget, and how external and internal state work in Flutter

For a deeper understanding let us start with stateless widget.

For more Flutter related Articles and Resources

Stateless widget is a widget that cannot re-run the build() method when its properties change.

Well, if the above statement doesn't make any sense, try to think this way.

When a stateless widget receives External data or Input data through its Constructor it re-runs the build() method.

As a result, it re-renders the UI. In the above diagram we have shown this.

However it's not true for stateless widget properties. In a stateless widget we can change its property by pressing a RaisedButton.

Pressing the button will change the property, it will change from 0 to 1 and from 1 to 2.

But, it cannot re-run the build() method and as a result it cannot re-render the UI.

Moreover, for this reason, we cannot see any change on the screen. Still we want to test this on an application.

The following examples will help us to understand this theoretical concept.

Stateless widget flutter Example

Let us consider a very simple example where user presses a button and that will increase the number shown above the button.

As the user presses the button, it increases the number in the Debug Console, like this:

I/flutter (5093): 1 I/flutter (5093): 2 I/flutter (5093): 3

Run the code in your IDE, you can clearly see the output. However it does not reflect on the screen. It doesn't re-run the build() method and re-renders the UI.

Why does it happen like this?

Because we tried to change the state through internal state or local data. Since that was the property of the widget class it didn't work.

What is build method in Flutter?

Let us see how the build() method works in Flutter. Above all, the build() method passes a 'context' that points where the Widget actually stays in the Widget tree.

A code snippet will help understand the role of this super-important method in Flutter.

```
1 import 'package:flutter/material.dart';
2
```

```
 3 void main() {
 4 runApp(OurApp());
 5 }
 6
 7 class OurApp extends StatelessWidget {
 8 @override
 9 Widget build(BuildContext context) {
10 return MaterialApp(
11 title: 'Our App',
12 debugShowCheckedModeBanner: false,
13 home: Scaffold(
14 body: ACenterClass(),
15 ),
16 );
17 }
18 }
```

Inside the "ACenterClass" widget we will use a property and method. Using Callback function to that method the RaisedButton named parameter 'onPress' will call that function.

Each time we press the button our debug console will show that the number is increasing. However, since it cannot re-run the build() method, our app cannot re-render the UI and we cannot see that increased number on the screen

```
 1 class ACenterClass extends StatelessWidget {
 2 var pressRemoteCount = 0;
 3 void pressRemote() {
 4 pressRemoteCount = pressRemoteCount + 1;
 5 print(pressRemoteCount);
 6 }
 7
 8 @override
 9 Widget build(BuildContext context) {
10 return Center(
11 child: Container(
12 alignment: Alignment.center,
13 width: 350.00,
14 height: 100.00,
15 decoration: BoxDecoration(
16 color: Colors.blue,
17 border: Border.all(
18 color: Colors.deepOrange,
19 width: 2.0,
20 style: BorderStyle.solid,
21 ),
22 borderRadius: BorderRadius.all(Radius.circular(40.0)),
23 boxShadow: [
24 BoxShadow(
25 color: Colors.black54,
```

```
26 blurRadius: 20.0,
27 spreadRadius: 20.0,
28 ),
29 ],
30 gradient: LinearGradient(
31 begin: Alignment.centerLeft,
32 end: Alignment.centerRight,
33 colors: [
34 Colors.red,
35 Colors.white,
36 ],
37 ),
38
39 ),
40 child: Column(
41 children: [
42 Text(
43 '$pressRemoteCount',
44 style: TextStyle(
45 fontSize: 30.0,
46 color: Colors.blue,
47 ),
48 ),
49 SizedBox(
50 height: 10.0,
51 ),
52 RaisedButton(
53 child: Text(
54 'Press Button',
55 style: TextStyle(
56 fontSize: 30.0,
57 color: Colors.blue,
58 ),
59 ),
60 onPressed: pressRemote,
61 ),
62 ],
63 ),
64 ),
65 );
66 }
67 }
```

Quite apart from the decoration, the real important piece of code is this:

```
1 var pressRemoteCount = 0;
2
3 void pressRemote() {
4
5 pressRemoteCount = pressRemoteCount + 1;
```

```
6
7 print(pressRemoteCount);
8
9 }
```

However, since pressing the button does not re-run the build() method, we don't see the value of the property 'pressRemoteCount' in the Text widget.

```
1 Text(
2
3 '$pressRemoteCount',
4
5 style: TextStyle( fontSize: 30.0, color: Colors.blue,
6
7 ),
```

Now, as we refactor the same code and change it to the stateful widget, it works.

How do you rebuild widgets in Flutter?

Having a stateful widget will keep track of the build method.

We can manage the internal state of the widget through class property. The next image will show you how we can see the counter value on the screen. Pressing the button will keep increasing the number.

Figure 2.2 – Going to change the internal state through Stateful Widget class property

Not only that, as the internal data or property's value changes it re-runs the build() method and that in turn will re-render the UI.

And, as a result, we see that the counter value increases with the pressing of the button. The next image will show you the same effect.

```dart
 1 class ACenterClass extends StatefulWidget {
 2 @override
 3 _ACenterClassState createState() => _ACenterClassState();
 4 }
 5
 6 class _ACenterClassState extends State<ACenterClass> {
 7 var pressRemoteCount = 0;
 8
 9 void pressRemote() {
10 setState(() {
11 pressRemoteCount = pressRemoteCount + 1;
12 });
13 }
14
15 @override
16 Widget build(BuildContext context) {
17 return Center(
18 child: Container(
19 alignment: Alignment.center,
20 width: 350.00,
21 height: 100.00,
22 decoration: BoxDecoration(
23 color: Colors.blue,
24 border: Border.all(
25 color: Colors.deepOrange,
26 width: 2.0,
27 style: BorderStyle.solid,
28 ),
29 borderRadius: BorderRadius.all(Radius.circular(40.0)),
30 boxShadow: [
31 BoxShadow(
32 color: Colors.black54,
33 blurRadius: 20.0,
34 spreadRadius: 20.0,
35 ),
36 ],
37 gradient: LinearGradient(
38 begin: Alignment.centerLeft,
39 end: Alignment.centerRight,
40 colors: [
41 Colors.red,
42 Colors.white,
43 ],
44 ),
45
46 ),
47 child: Column(
48 children: [
49 Text(
50 '$pressRemoteCount',
```

```
51 style: TextStyle(
52 fontSize: 30.0,
53 color: Colors.blue,
54 ),
55 ),
56 SizedBox(
57 height: 10.0,
58 ),
59 RaisedButton(
60 child: Text(
61 'Press Button',
62 style: TextStyle(
63 fontSize: 30.0,
64 color: Colors.blue,
65 ),
66 ),
67 onPressed: pressRemote,
68 ),
69 ],
70 ),
71 ),
72 );
73 }
74 }
```

In the above code snippet, this part is important and makes the difference:

```
1 class ACenterClass extends StatefulWidget {
2 @override
3 _ACenterClassState createState() => _ACenterClassState();
4 }
5
6 class _ACenterClassState extends State<ACenterClass> {
7 var pressRemoteCount = 0;
8
9 void pressRemote() {
10 setState(() {
11 pressRemoteCount = pressRemoteCount + 1;
12 });
13 }
14
15 @override
16 Widget build(BuildContext context) {
17 return Center(
18
19 ....
```

Now, inside the Center widget we have our Text widget and RaisedButton widget as before. Nonetheless, the re-rendered UI reflects the change. And now it shows the increased value.

Figure 2.3 – The re-rendered UI reflects the change, and now it shows the increased value

As the internal data changes, it re-runs the build() method and the UI gets re-rendered in Flutter stateful widget

When Should I call setState Flutter?

As we have seen in the stateless widget, without the setState() method the widget does change the property value. Remember the debug console output, which indicated that the property value was increased by the press of the RaisedButton widget.

However, that could not re-run the build() method which was necessary to re-render the UI so the user could see the change.

Hence the updates were not reflected on the screen.

Therefore use setState to cause a rebuild of the widget and its descendants. The build() will re-run anyway. And exactly that happens in the stateful widget.

In the stateful widget the setState plays as a trigger that informs Flutter to re-run the build() method so the descendant Text widget, which stores the property value, will get rebuilt.

For more Flutter related Articles and Resources

3. What is callback in Flutter? How do you pass a function in Flutter?

We are going to discuss two things in this Chapter 3. Flutter enthusiasts often want to know what is callback in Flutter?

Along with it, comes another important question, how do you pass a function in Flutter?

In addition to these questions we'll also try to understand what is callback.

For more Flutter related Articles and Resources

What is callback?

In computer programming we pass functions as argument to other code. We give a name to this type of action – callback.

Why?

Because at some convenient time the 'other code' will call back or execute the argument.

Let's see how it takes place in flutter.

In a stateful widget, consider a function like this:

```
1 void _answerQuestion() {
2 setState(() {
3 _questionIndex = _questionIndex + 1;
4 });
5 if (_questionIndex > 1) {
6 _questionIndex = 0;
7 }
8 }
```

Inside a RaisedButton we can call back this function like this:

```
1 onPressed: _answerQuestion,
```

The synchronous callback tells the machine don't wait, invoke it immediately. However, the asynchronous callback likes to wait and invokes it later time.

What is callback in Flutter?

In flutter we often use callback when we want to change simple values using stateful widget. As we have just seen above.

If we see the whole piece of code and see the image of our app, it will spill the beans.

What I'm going to do? Well, let me tell you that. We're going to build a simple quiz app. The user views a question in text and below that question, he'll find three answer buttons.

Clicking any button takes her to the next question.

In the main dart file we have the first piece of code, like this:

```
 1 import 'package:flutter/material.dart';
 2
 3 void main() {
 4 runApp(QuizApp());
 5 }
 6
 7 class QuizApp extends StatelessWidget {
 8 @override
 9 Widget build(BuildContext context) {
10 return MaterialApp(
11 title: 'Quiz App',
12 debugShowCheckedModeBanner: false,
13 home: FirstPage(),
14 );
15 }
16 }
```

Next, we must define the FirstPage widget. It should be a stateful widget. Otherwise we cannot change the state by clicking the buttons.

Here is the next part of code:

```
 1 class FirstPage extends StatefulWidget {
 2 @override
 3 _FirstPageState createState() => _FirstPageState();
 4 }
 5
 6 class _FirstPageState extends State<FirstPage> {
 7 var _questionIndex = 0;
 8
 9 void _answerQuestion() {
10 setState(() {
11 _questionIndex = _questionIndex + 1;
12 });
13 if (_questionIndex > 1) {
14 _questionIndex = 0;
15 }
16 }
17
18 var _questions = [
19 'What is your favorite book?',
20 'Who is your favorite author?',
21 ];
22
23 @override
24 Widget build(BuildContext context) {
25 return Scaffold(
```

```
26 appBar: AppBar(),
27 body: Container(
28 width: double.infinity,
29 padding: EdgeInsets.all(
30 20.0,
31 ),
32 margin: EdgeInsets.all(
33 10.0,
34 ),
35 child: Center(
36 child: Column(
37 children: [
38 Text(
39 _questions[_questionIndex],
40 style: TextStyle(
41 color: Colors.red,
42 fontSize: 20,
43 ),
44 ),
45 RaisedButton(
46 child: Text('Answer 1'),
47 color: Colors.blue,
48 onPressed: _answerQuestion,
49 ),
50 RaisedButton(
51 child: Text('Answer 2'),
52 color: Colors.blue,
53 onPressed: _answerQuestion,
54 ),
55 RaisedButton(
56 child: Text('Answer 3'),
57 color: Colors.blue,
58 onPressed: _answerQuestion,
59 ),
60 ],
61 ),
62 ),
63 ),
64 );
65 }
66 }
```

Now, we have our simple quiz application ready.

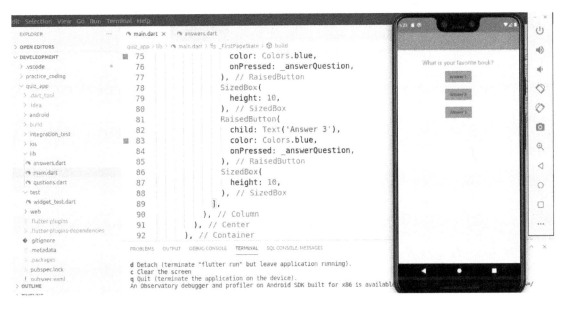

Figure 3.1 – A minimalist Quiz App

If we click any answer button that will take us to the next question.

However, flutter doesn't like such congestion. We've written the whole application in a single file. Whereas we could have separated them, and kept them in separate directories.

We'll come to that point in a minute.

How do you call widgets in Flutter?

As we have seen in the above code, there are two different parts. One is question that reflects on the Text widget. And the other part is answers, which reflect on button.

Flutter encourages you to pass down the state of a child as constructor parameters.

So let's create two child-widgets in two separate files like this. The first one is questions.dart:

```
1 import 'package:flutter/material.dart';
2
3 class Questions extends StatelessWidget {
4 final String handler;
5 Questions(this.handler);
6 @override
7 Widget build(BuildContext context) {
8 return Text(
9 handler,
10 style: TextStyle(
11 color: Colors.red,
12 fontSize: 20,
13 ),
```

```
14 );
15 }
16 }
```

Through the Questions constructor we have passed a string handler.

And the other is answers.dart, and the code is like this:

```
 1 import 'package:flutter/material.dart';
 2
 3 class Answers extends StatelessWidget {
 4 final String yourAnswer;
 5 final Function answerQuestion;
 6 Answers(this.yourAnswer, this.answerQuestion);
 7 @override
 8 Widget build(BuildContext context) {
 9 return RaisedButton(
10 child: Text(yourAnswer),
11 color: Colors.blue,
12 onPressed: answerQuestion,
13 );
14 }
15 }
```

Here we need to pass two arguments through Answers constructor. One is text or string. And the other is a function. We'll call this function back later in our main file.

So let's have a look at the final piece of code.

In the main file, we should import these two child-widgets first.

```
 1 import 'package:quiz_app/answers.dart';
 2 import 'package:quiz_app/questions.dart';
 3
 4 Next inside the build() method we will change our previous code to
this:
 5
 6 @override
 7 Widget build(BuildContext context) {
 8 return Scaffold(
 9 appBar: AppBar(),
10 body: Container(
11 width: double.infinity,
12 padding: EdgeInsets.all(
13 20.0,
14 ),
15 margin: EdgeInsets.all(
16 10.0,
17 ),
18 child: Center(
19 child: Column(
```

```
20 children: [
21 Questions(_questions[_questionIndex]),
22 SizedBox(
23 height: 10,
24 ),
25 Answers('Answer 1', _answerQuestion),
26 Answers('Answer 2', _answerQuestion),
27 Answers('Answer 3', _answerQuestion),
28 ],
29 ),
30 ),
31 ),
32 );
33 }
```

There is no change in our simple quiz app. Except that the RaisedButton widgets get closer to each other, it looks like before.

Since we have removed the SizedBox widget in between RaisedButton widgets, they get a little bit closer. Nonetheless our quiz app is working like before.

We have successfully passed around the callback in Flutter through Class constructors.

For more Flutter related Articles and Resources

4. What is a map in Flutter? How do you map a list in Flutter?

Before you start reading this Chpater 4 on list, and map examples, you should know how we use list in Flutter. Moreover, you must know the primary concepts of data structure in dart programming language. That also includes map.

Once you know how we use list in dart, or what is map in dart, it becomes easy to understand the main topic of this article.

We're going to discuss what is a map in Flutter? Not only that, we will also discuss in detail how we can map a list in Flutter.

In the previous chapter where we had discussed what is callback in flutter, and how do you pass a function in flutter, we also touched on a key concept of state management.

For more Flutter related Articles and Resources

What is the key concept of State Management in Flutter?

** We cannot change the state of a stateless widget through its property, although we can change the state externally. **

Specially when we pass the external data through its constructor.

Based on that assumption we have created two custom widgets Answers and Questions. Through Answers constructor, we pass two parameters – one is a function, and the other is a string data type.

At the same time, we have also created another custom widget Questions that has only one external data to be passed. And that is string.

What is a map in Flutter?

Map is a list of elements where we arrange the elements in a key, value pair. Normally in a list of items what do we see?

There is always an index that starts from 0, and through that index we can get the value. In a map, through the key, we get the value. As a result we use different types of methods in map. Moreover, we can also include a map in our list, and vice versa.

Exactly that happens here.

Let us see two custom widgets first.

```
 1 import 'package:flutter/material.dart';
 2
 3 class Answers extends StatelessWidget {
 4 final String yourAnswer;
 5 final Function answerQuestion;
 6 Answers(this.yourAnswer, this.answerQuestion);
 7 @override
 8 Widget build(BuildContext context) {
 9 return RaisedButton(
10 child: Text(
11 yourAnswer,
12 style: TextStyle(
13 color: Colors.white,
14 fontSize: 30,
15 fontWeight: FontWeight.bold,
16 ),
17 ),
18 color: Colors.blue,
19 onPressed: answerQuestion,
20 );
21 }
22 }
```

The Answers custom widget returns a RaisedButton widget that has a child widget Text and another named parameter onPressed, which returns a void function.

For that reason, we have to pass two parameters through Answers constructor. One is string and the other is a function.

Next we see the other custom widget Questions.

```
 1 import 'package:flutter/material.dart';
 2
 3 class Questions extends StatelessWidget {
 4 final String handler;
 5 Questions(this.handler);
 6 @override
 7 Widget build(BuildContext context) {
 8 return Text(
 9 handler,
10 style: TextStyle(
11 color: Colors.red,
12 fontSize: 40,
13 fontWeight: FontWeight.bold,
14 ),
15 );
16 }
17 }
```

The constructor passes a string.

How do you map a list in Flutter?

That is the main challenge. Inside our main function, we have a combination of list and map, in this way:

```
 1 var _questions = [
 2 {
 3 'questionText': 'What\'s the meaning of Assuetude?',
 4 'answers': ['kiss', 'insolent', 'habit', 'half'],
 5 },
 6 {
 7 'questionText': 'What\'s the meaning of Disingenuous?',
 8 'answers': ['guilty', 'jovial', 'jocular', 'insincere'],
 9 },
10 {
11 'questionText': 'What\'s the meaning of Afflatus?',
12 'answers': ['ghost', 'inspiration', 'lifeless', 'greedy'],
13 },
14 ];
```

The great advantage of our above code is that inside the "_questions" list we have accommodated the answers also.

The next challenge is we should be able to view the next question by clicking the correct answer. Just like this:

How did we do that?

Let us see the Center widget:

```
 1 child: Center(
 2 child: Column(
 3 children: [
 4 Questions(
 5 _questions[_questionIndex]['questionText'],
 6 ),
 7 ...(_questions[_questionIndex]['answers'] as List<String>)
 8 .map((answer) {
 9 return Answers(answer, _answerQuestion);
10 }).toList()
11 ],
12 ),
13 ),
```

We have used three dots "…" operator to extend the collection.

Why we should do that? Because we're insie a collection, that is Column children, which returns a List of collections.

Now we have successfully mapped the answers to the list of questions.

For more Flutter related Articles and Resources

5. Why is state management in Flutter? What is flutter state?

Why state management in Flutter is one of the most important topics? What is flutter state?

Well, state is the information that a user can read synchronously with the change in widget. During the lifetime of the widget, it can hold that data.

Even if you refresh or render the widget, the data stays.

Now, there are different types of approaches to manage state.

This is the most basic approach. Moreover, in this tutorial, we will see how a widget can manage the state and renders the state to itself. Why do we need state management?

To begin with, I must clarify one thing. State is an object. It is not a widget. Although in Flutter, everything is widget.

Therefore, we can say that a StatefulWidget is actually immutable, it is StatelessWidget. The State of the widget is managed by the State object.

However, that is not the key point here.

We'll see how a widget can manage its own state.

There are a few steps that we need to do before we proceed.

We'll create a class OwnStateManagingWidget. And we'll manages state for OwnStateManagingWidget.

Next, we'll define the _stateChanged boolean which determines the box's current color.

Next, we'll define the _changeState() function, which updates _stateChanged when the box is tapped and calls the setState() function to update the UI. At the end, we'll implement all interactive behavior for the widget.

For more Flutter related Articles and Resources

How we change the widget state in Flutter?

We've defined the _stateChanged boolean which determines the box's current color. And we've defined the _changeState() function, too.

Let us see the code, so we can understand how it works.

```
1 import 'package:flutter/material.dart';
2
3 class OwnStateManagingWidget extends StatefulWidget {
4 @override
5 _OwnStateManagingWidgetState createState() =>
_OwnStateManagingWidgetState();
6 }
7
8 class _OwnStateManagingWidgetState extends
State<OwnStateManagingWidget> {
9 /// let's define the boolean value first
10 ///
11
12 bool _stateChanged = false;
13
14 /// let's create a function that will define the setState() method
15 /// it'll change the state of this widget only
16 ///
17 void _changeState() {
18 setState(() {
19 _stateChanged = !_stateChanged;
20 });
21 }
22
23 @override
24 Widget build(BuildContext context) {
25 /// we'll use GestureDetector so that we can tap a box that will
turn green as
26 /// the state is changed
27 return GestureDetector(
28 /// when we tap this onTap fires
29 onTap: _changeState,
```

```
30 child: Container(
31 child: Center(
32 child: Text(
33 _stateChanged ? 'State Changed' : 'State Unchanged',
34 style: TextStyle(fontSize: 35.0),
35 ),
36 ),
37 width: 350.0,
38 height: 350.0,
39 decoration:
40 BoxDecoration(color: _stateChanged ? Colors.green : Colors.red),
41 ),
42 );
43 }
44 }
```

How does it work? The _changeState() function, updates _stateChanged boolean value to true when the box is tapped.

Once the user taps the red box, it calls the setState() function to update the UI and make the box color to green.

Figure 5.1 – Tapping the box will change the color

How to manage state of child through parent widget?

Any flutter widget can manage its own state. It uses stateful widget. However,when it's a stateless child widget, the parent manages its state.

It's an interesting feature of Flutter. Especially when we manage state in a small application.

For a large scale application where we have to pass the state object to many screens, or pages, this process is not good. In such cases we'll use Provider or Riverpod. Even we can use the BLOC architecture.

However, Provider is our best option. And we must stick to one good choice.

Still, to understand Flutter state management, you should know how it works at the root level.

How do you use stateful widget Flutter?

A Flutter stateful widget is a dynamic widget. As the user taps a box, or click a button, it changes its state. And this process updates the whole widget.

A stateful widget depends either on user action, or on data change.

The State class, or object actually manages the internal state of the stateful widget. In that sense, a stateful widget also depends on the State class, which is not a widget.

In this tutorial, we will see how a stateful parent widget manages the state of a stateless child widget.

If you've not read the previous article on how a widget manages its own state, please read it, before we start.

How a Child Widget exports its state to its parent

How can a Child Widget export its state to its parent? Without a callback, we cannot imagine it.

So, we need to think about the callback first. Since the parent is importing the state of the child widget, we don't have to make the child widget stateful anymore. It can be stateless.

However, the parent widget should be stateful. Moreover, there should be a consistent mechanism that will help the child widget to export its state safely.

Let's see the code of the Parent Widget class.

```
1 class ParentWidget extends StatefulWidget {
2 @override
3 _ParentWidgetState createState() => _ParentWidgetState();
4 }
5
6 class _ParentWidgetState extends State<ParentWidget> {
7 /// Manages the _inActive state for ChildWidget.
8 ///
9 bool _inActive = true;
10
11 /// Implements _manageStateForChildWidget(), the method called when
the box is tappe\
```

```
12 d.
13 ///
14 void _manageStateForChildWidget(bool newValue) {
15 setState(() {
16 _inActive = newValue;
17 });
18 }
19
20 @override
21 Widget build(BuildContext context) {
22 return ChildWidget(
23 inActive: _inActive,
24 notifyParent: _manageStateForChildWidget,
25 );
26 }
27 }
```

The code is very straight forward. By default the state object should be inactive. So we've made it true. It also manages the state of the child widget.

As we tap a box, it will no longer remain inactive. It becomes false, from true and makes the state active.

So we need the setState() method, that will implement a method, which in turn,passes a boolean parameter whose value is false.

Figure 5.2 – Tapping box turns the box green

Watch this part of the above code:

```
 1 /// Manages the _inActive state for ChildWidget.
 2 ///
 3 bool _inActive = true;
 4
 5 /// Implements _manageStateForChildWidget(), the method called when
the box is tappe\
 6 d.
 7 ///
 8 void _manageStateForChildWidget(bool newValue) {
 9 setState(() {
10 _inActive = newValue;
11 });
12 }
```

Now, we need a callback.

For that we will use a special feature of Flutter:

```
1 typedef ValueChanged<T> = void Function(T value);
```

How Child Widget implements this special property?

Let us see the code of Child Widget. That will explain the rest.

```
 1 /// Extends StatelessWidget because all state is handled by its
parent, ParentWidget
 2 ///
 3 class ChildWidget extends StatelessWidget {
 4 ChildWidget({Key key, this.inActive = true, this.notifyParent})
 5 : super(key: key);
 6 final bool inActive;
 7
 8 /// When a tap is detected, it notifies the parent.
 9 ///
10 final ValueChanged<bool> notifyParent;
11 void manageState() {
12 notifyParent(!inActive);
13 }
14
15 @override
16 Widget build(BuildContext context) {
17 return GestureDetector(
18 onTap: manageState,
19 child: Container(
20 child: Center(
21 child: Text(
22 inActive ? 'Inactive' : 'Active',
23 style: TextStyle(
24 fontSize: 25.0,
25 color: Colors.white,
26 ),
```

```
27 ),
28 ),
29 width: 250.0,
30 height: 250.0,
31 decoration: BoxDecoration(color: inActive ? Colors.red :
Colors.green),
32 ),
33 );
34 }
35 }
```

Watch this part of the above code:

```
1 /// When a tap is detected, it notifies the parent.
2 ///
3 final ValueChanged<bool> notifyParent;
4
5 void manageState() {
6 notifyParent(!inActive);
7 }
```

As we have said earlier, using this special feature of Flutter, we have a method, which passes a boolean value that in turn exports the state to the parent widget.

How the export and import of state take place

How does the child widget export state? And, at the same time, how does the parent widget import the state?

The mystery reveals itself at the child widget constructor, where two named parameters point to a piece of data and a method that through its parameter change the state of that data.

At the parent widget:

```
1 return ChildWidget( inActive: _inActive, notifyParent:
_manageStateForChildWidget, );
```

And at the child widget, this line is important.

```
1 final ValueChanged<bool> notifyParent;
```

Here notifyParent is a method that passes a certain type of data. We have indicated which type of data should be passed –

```
1 ValueChanged<bool>.
```

For more Flutter related Articles and Resources

6. How many types of widgets are there in Flutter?

There are two types of widgets in Flutter – stateful and stateless. However, again we should broadly categorize them into two types – visible and invisible.

Before we start discusiing Inherited Widget, let us take a brief look at the inside world of Widgets.

For more Flutter related Articles and Resources

What are visible widgets?

The widgets that we can see. The widgets that take inputs and give outputs.

```
1 RaisedButton() and Text(), etc...
```

As we will see in a minute.

Yet, Invisible widgets also play crucial roles. Because they control the look and structure of the body of the Flutter app.

```
1 Row(), Column(), ListView(), etc...
```

The Container() widget may belong to both categories. Why so? As we can decorate the container giving it color, or changing its shape. We can also make it invisible by only placing other visible widgets inside it.

The Container() widget lets you create a rectangular visual element.

We will see the examples of such widgets in a minute.

What are the widgets in Flutter?

Widgets, as a whole, control the view of any flutter app.

We build our UI out of widgets. That is why we say in Flutter, widget is everything. However, that is partially true. There are classes like State that is not widget in nature. Although it takes the most important role in managing the state of any Flutter app.

When a widget changes its state, or we use a stateful widget, the widget rebuilds its description.

Visible and invisible, both types of widgets help each other to describe how the view of the app should look like. How do you use widgets in Flutter?

In the following example we will see a simple app that will return a text in the center of the app body.

```
1 void main() {
2 runApp(
3 Center(
```

```
 4 child: Text(
 5 'Hello, world!',
 6 style: TextStyle(
 7 fontSize: 30.0,
 8 fontWeight: FontWeight.bold,
 9 ),
10 textDirection: TextDirection.ltr,
11 ),
12 ),
13 );
14 }
```

The simple code, displayed above, will render only a text "Hello World" on the screen.

We have used only two widgets. Center() and Text(). The Center() widget belongs to the type of the invisible widget. And the Text() widget belongs to the type of the visible widget.

Since the root widget is Center(), the framework forces the root widget to cover the whole screen. As a result, the Text() widget, which is the branch of this small widget tree, ends up centered.

We had to specify the text direction also. However if we had used MaterialApp widget, we would not have to think about those small nitty-gritty. MaterialApp would take care of that.

How do I create a Custom widget in Flutter?

While writing an app, we should plan what type of widgets we're going to write. As we have said earlier, the widgets will either inherit from stateful,or stateless widgets.

As of now, we are not going to maintain state. So our widgets will be sub-classes of stateless widget.

Now the code changes making our small app presentable.

```
 1 import 'package:flutter/material.dart';
 2
 3 void main() {
 4 runApp(OurApp());
 5 }
 6
 7 class OurApp extends StatelessWidget {
 8 @override
 9 Widget build(BuildContext context) {
10 return MaterialApp(
11 title: 'Our App',
12 debugShowCheckedModeBanner: false,
13 home: Scaffold(
```

```
14 body: Center(
15 child: Text(
16 'Hello, world!',
17 style: TextStyle(
18 fontSize: 30.0,
19 fontWeight: FontWeight.bold,
20 ),
21 textDirection: TextDirection.ltr,
22 ),
23 ),
24 ),
25 );
26 }
27 }
```

However, we have used the default Scaffold widget that controls the whole body of the app.

We could have written our own Scaffold, which will actually render a material design in the same manner.

Let us check this new code snippet, where we have just written our own piece of custom Scaffold widget.

```
1 import 'package:flutter/material.dart';
2
3 void main() {
4 runApp(OurApp());
5 }
6
7 class OurApp extends StatelessWidget {
8 @override
9 Widget build(BuildContext context) {
10 return MaterialApp(
11 title: 'Our App',
12 debugShowCheckedModeBanner: false,
13 home: OurScaffold(),
14 );
15 }
16 }
17
18 class OurScaffold extends StatelessWidget {
19 @override
20 Widget build(BuildContext context) {
21 // It creates a piece of material dsign
22 return Material(
23 // Column is a vertical, linear layout.
24 child: Column(
25 children: <Widget>[
26 Expanded(
```

```
27 child: Center(
28 child: Text(
29 'Hello, world!',
30 style: TextStyle(
31 fontSize: 30.0,
32 fontWeight: FontWeight.bold,
33 color: Colors.redAccent,
34 ),
35 ),
36 ),
37 ),
38 ],
39 ),
40 );
41 }
42 }
```

We have only changed the color of the text to show the difference.

```
1 color: Colors.redAccent,
```

For more Flutter related Articles and Resources

7. What is inherited widget in Flutter, how do you use state management?

The inherited widget is one of the low level process of state management in Flutter. However, when it manages state, it also propagates information down the tree.

And to do that it acts as a base class. Although state management is a complex topic, it can be managed quite comfortably through Inherited Widgets.

In this Chapter, let us concentrate on InheritedWidget only, as this is extremely important concept in Flutter. Especially if you want to manage state efficiently.

However, before proceeding further, let's check a diagram so it will clearly depict us how state can be floated to the bottom-most widget without affecting the parent widgets.

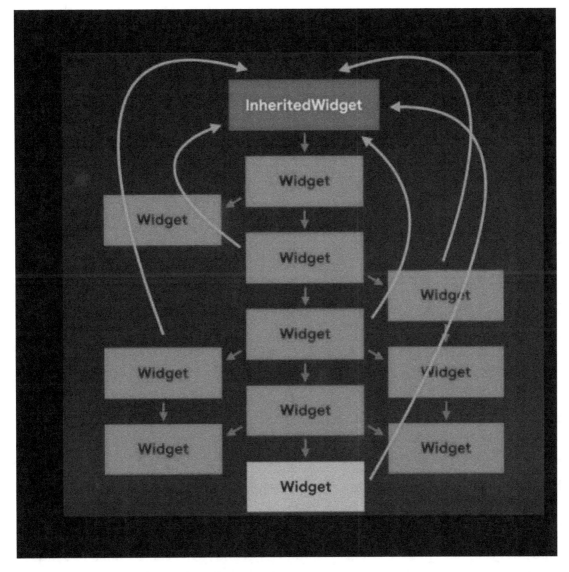

Figure 7.1 – How Inherited Widget works

We should remember that Flutter is all about widgets.

Flutter builds tree and sub-tree of widgets to build an application. Think about a family tree structure. Flutter builds its widgets in that fashion.

For more Flutter related Articles and Resources

What is InheritedWidget in Flutter?

We can answer the above question in one or two sentences. InheritedWidget is a special type of widget that defines a context at the root of the base tree. This context then travels down the sub-tree as deep as possible.

However, the advantage is plenty. The lowest widget at the sub-tree may directly access the state defined in the InheritedWidget without affecting the other widgets residing above it.

By using the InheritedWidget when the lowest level widget, residing at the bottom of the widget tree, tries to change its state, that process does not affect other widgets above.

It does not happen if we use widget specific another low-level approach 'setState' that comes with Flutter naturally. Although it adds interactivity to any Flutter app in a safe way, but while doing so it redraws every widget above it in the widget tree.

We don't prefer that approach. For a small application we can use that approach though.

How do you manage state efficiently?

In a complex scenario, where we need to pass state using the widget specific low-level approach 'setState' among hundreds of widgets, it becomes cumbersome.

The InheritedWidget tries to solve that riddle in its own way, although it has some disadvantages too. We will come to that point in a minute.

Before that let us take a look at an image to get an idea of how InheritedWidget works.

InheritedWidget manages state efficiently, but is that all?

No. As I have said earlier, I want to emphasize on the word "context". In the above image you see that some widgets below the sub-tree talks directly to the InheritedWidget residing at the root of the widget tree.

The context flows down to the bottom-most-widget without affecting other. When the InheritedWidget changes its state it passes the new value to the consumer bottom-most-widget.

While doing so the InheritedWidget rebuilds itself and at the same time it rebuilds its consumer.

In doing so Flutter does not rebuild the other top-widgets through which the context flows down to the bottom.

How do you use an inherited widget in Flutter?

Let us come to the point. How can we use InheritedWidget in Flutter?

We need write a widget tree first. The tree starts with two InheritedWidget. One passes the color through its context. And the other passes an integer value through its context.

Let us see the main method through which we run our InheritedWidget app. You get the full code snippets at my GitHub repo.

```
1 import 'package:flutter/material.dart';
2 import 'controller/inherited-widget/inherited_widget_on_top.dart';
```

```
 3
 4 main() => runApp(OurApp());
 5
 6 class OurApp extends StatelessWidget {
 7 @override
 8 Widget build(BuildContext context) {
 9 return MaterialApp(
10 title: 'Our App',
11 debugShowCheckedModeBanner: false,
12 home: Scaffold(
13 body: InheritedWidgetOnTop(),
14 ),
15 );
16 }
17 }
```

Flutter widget tree can be deep, very deep

Keeping the above philosophy in our mind, we need to at the base of the tree keeps our two inherited widgets.

```
 1 import 'package:flutter/material.dart';
 2 import 'package:our_app/controller/inherited-widget/widgets-
lists/widgets_lists.dart\
 3 ';
 4
 5 class InheritedWidgetOnTop extends StatefulWidget {
 6 @override
 7 _InheritedWidgetOnTopState createState() =>
_InheritedWidgetOnTopState();
 8 }
 9
10 class _InheritedWidgetOnTopState extends State<InheritedWidgetOnTop>
{
11 @override
12 Widget build(BuildContext context) {
13 return ListView(
14 padding: const EdgeInsets.all(30.0),
15 children: [
16 EyeColor(
17 color: Colors.deepOrange,
18 child: Builder(builder: (BuildContext innerContext) {
19 return GrandParent();
20 })),
21 SizedBox(
22 height: 10.0,
23 ),
24 ChangingAge(
25 age: new ChangeAge(age: 25),
26 child: Builder(builder: (BuildContext textContext) {
```

```
27 return UncleClasses();
28 })),
29 ],
30 );
31 }
32 }
```

Two inherited widgets are "EyeColor" and "ChangingAge".

Through the "EyeColor"we pass a context that carries the color of eyes. The descendant widgets, hopefully they are humans, will consume the context and get their eye colors accordingly.

However, any descendant may not wish to consume that context, and choose its own eye color.

The above code clearly indicates that the consumer of the inherited widget "EyeColor" is the Grandparent widget. The Grandparent widget has FatherClass widget as sub-tree.

To make it simple, we have another inherited widget "ChangingAge" that has also a consumer widget "UncleClasses". The "UncleClasses" widget has a fairly deep sub-tree, in which we have two uncles widgets of different age. One of the uncle has a child, so we can view that child as the bottom-most-widget in the Uncles tree.

Moreover, we can change the age of each uncle. We can change the age of the child too by pressing buttons.

Nevertheless age changes when we press the button, the context maintains the state so efficiently that the other ages do not get affected.

We keep our inherited widgets in a separate folders

Let us break down our app structure a little bit.

Inside our "lib" folder, the folder structure looks like the following:

```
1 controller/inherited-widget/widgets-lists/widgets_lists.dart
```

Now the widget lists include these two inherited widgets.

```
 1 import 'package:flutter/material.dart';
 2
 3 class EyeColor extends InheritedWidget {
 4 const EyeColor({
 5 Key key,
 6 @required this.color,
 7 @required Widget child,
 8 }) : assert(color != null),
 9 assert(child != null),
10 super(key: key, child: child);
11
```

```
12 final Color color;
13
14 static EyeColor of(BuildContext context) {
15 return context.dependOnInheritedWidgetOfExactType<EyeColor>();
16 }
17
18 @override
19 bool updateShouldNotify(EyeColor old) => color != old.color;
20 }
21
22 class ChangingAge extends InheritedWidget {
23 const ChangingAge({
24 Key key,
25 @required this.age,
26 @required Widget child,
27 }) : assert(age != null),
28 super(key: key, child: child);
29
30 final ChangeAge age;
31
32 static ChangingAge of(BuildContext context) {
33 return context.dependOnInheritedWidgetOfExactType<ChangingAge>();
34 }
35
36 @override
37 bool updateShouldNotify(ChangingAge old) => age != old.age;
38 }
39
40 class ChangeAge {
41 int age;
42 ChangeAge({this.age});
43 void changeAge() {
44 age += 5;
45 }
46 }
```

How does Scope matter in passing Context?

Yes, that's a valid point. While building this simple app, we should remember that in the widget tree there could be a lot of widgets that do not consume the same context.

So there could be widgets that may not in the Scope. The value that context carries on its shoulder will be null for those widgets that are not in the Scope. Otherwise the context carries a default value.

It is as simple as that.

Taking a look at the above code will tell you that there is a static "of" method that passes "context" as a parameter. And it returns the following line of code:

```
1 return context.dependOnInheritedWidgetOfExactType<ChangingAge>();
```

It allows the class to create its own fallback logic. It is important for one reason. There could be other widgets who are not consumers and they are not in the scope.

Now the "of" method may return any type of data. In our app, the inherited widget "EyeColor" returns Flutter Color class. The consumer widgets of inherited widget EyeColor

The Grandparent is the main consumer, and it has a descendant FatherClass. Let us close watch them first.

```
 1 class GrandParent extends StatelessWidget {
 2 @override
 3 Widget build(BuildContext context) {
 4 final eyeColor = EyeColor.of(context).color;
 5 return Column(
 6 children: [
 7 Text(
 8 'I am the Grandparent, although I am a Ghost now! I had two sons.',
 9 style: TextStyle(
10 fontWeight: FontWeight.bold,
11 fontSize: 25.0,
12 color: eyeColor,
13 ),
14 ),
15 SizedBox(
16 height: 10.0,
17 ),
18 FatherClass(),
19 ],
20 );
21 }
22 }
23
24 class FatherClass extends StatelessWidget {
25 @override
26 Widget build(BuildContext context) {
27 return Column(
28 children: [
29 Text(
30 'I am the Father. I have two brothers.',
31 style: TextStyle(
32 color: EyeColor.of(context).color,
33 fontSize: 30.0,
34 fontWeight: FontWeight.bold),
35 ),
36 ],
37 );
```

```
38 }
39 }
```

As you see on the above code, for Grandparent we have consumed the context this way:

```
1 final eyeColor = EyeColor.of(context).color;
```

And then we use that color indirectly.

```
1 color: eyeColor,
```

In the FatherClass widget we have consumed it directly. Since in our inherited widget EyeColor we have defined the color as deep orange. The text inside both consumer take the same color.

We have not finished our code snippets yet. We have another inherited widget "ChangingAge". Through the context an integer data, which is age of the uncles and the child, flows down to the bottom.

How do you manage state through inherited widgets?

Well, the next code snippets will show you that.

Managing state becomes fairly simple with the inherited widgets. The main consumer of the inherited widget "ChangingAge" is "UncleClasses".

Let us take a look at the code first.

```
 1 class UncleClasses extends StatelessWidget {
 2 @override
 3 Widget build(BuildContext context) {
 4 return Column(
 5 children: [
 6 Text('This is a list of Uncles with different states.',
 7 style: TextStyle(
 8 color: Colors.black45,
 9 fontSize: 25.0,
10 fontWeight: FontWeight.bold,
11 )),
12 SizedBox(
13 height: 5.0,
14 ),
15 FirstUncleClass(),
16 SizedBox(
17 height: 5.0,
18 ),
19 UncleClass(),
20 ],
21 );
```

```
22 }
23 }
```

The main consumer has two more consumer widgets inside it. FirstUncleClass and UncleClass.

Let us take a look at them too.

```
 1 class FirstUncleClass extends StatefulWidget {
 2 @override
 3 _FirstUncleClassState createState() => _FirstUncleClassState();
 4 }
 5
 6 class _FirstUncleClassState extends State<FirstUncleClass> {
 7 var firstUncleAge = new ChangeAge(age: 35);
 8 @override
 9 Widget build(BuildContext context) {
10 return Column(
11 children: [
12 Text(
13 'I am First Uncle, ${firstUncleAge.age} years old, change my age by
add button below\
14 .',
15 style: TextStyle(
16 fontSize: 30.0,
17 color: Colors.lightGreenAccent,
18 backgroundColor: Colors.black),
19 ),
20 SizedBox(
21 height: 10.0,
22 ),
23 FloatingActionButton(
24 onPressed: () {
25 setState(() {
26 firstUncleAge.changeAge();
27 });
28 },
29 child: Icon(Icons.add),
30 backgroundColor: Colors.blue,
31 ),
32 ],
33 );
34 }
35 }
```

If we press the FloatingActionButton below, the age of first uncle increases by 5. Probably he is in hurry to grow older.

The code of second uncle class is similar to that of the first uncle. However,the design slightly differs. Another important thing is this widget has a child. So we have declared it inside too.

Just below the FloatingActionButton .

```
1 FloatingActionButton(
2 onPressed: () {
3 setState(() {
4 secondUncleAge.changeAge();
5 });
6 },
7 child: Icon(Icons.add),
8 backgroundColor: Colors.blue,
9 ),
10 UnclesChildClass(),
```

The widget UnclesChildClass has the similar code structure, so we need not repeat it.

Press the FloatingActionButton, age of each consumer increases by 5 individually. As I have said earlier, the whole family is in hurry to grow older quickly. What about you?

Actually the same context, here age, flows down the family tree.

The context points to the exact position where any Widget stays at the Widget tree. We'll discuss this topic separately in another Chapter.

For more Flutter related Articles and Resources

8. What is flutter provider? How does provider flutter work?

What is Flutter provider? The answer will remain incomplete. Why? Because you must also know how provider flutter works.

Provider is a Flutter package. It's a wrapper around the InheritedWidget.

Before you proceed you must add the dependency on provider to the 'pubspec.yaml' file.

It looks like this:

```
1 // pubspec.yaml
2
3 dependencies:
4 flutter:
5 sdk: flutter
```

Now you are set to use Provider to manage state in your app.

What is state? Well, state is something that exists on memory. When your app is running, in most cases you will try to manage state. Provider helps you to do that.

State is extremely important. Managing it efficiently is important too.

Because to build any type of complex app that handles multiple screens, different variables, and user sessions, managing state is crucial, you should plan it beforehand.

Why?

Flutter creates a very deep and nested widget tree. To manage state at the lowest bottom, you cannot rebuild every top-widget. That is wasteful memory consumption.

Provider in Flutter is the answer!

Enough talking. Let us try to do some code together. Our goal is to understand the main concept of Flutter Provider.

Using ChangeNotifierProvider is one solution. It comes from the Provider package and it provides an instance of a ChangeNotifier to the widgets. Now Flutter has has in-built mechanisms for widgets to provide data and services to their distant descendants.

Widget is very powerful. ChangeNotifierProvider uses that power to notify the listeners.

How does it do that?

Making it possible needs to place it on top of our widget tree.

```
 1 import
'package:basic_flutter_provider/models/counting_the_number.dart';
 2 import 'package:basic_flutter_provider/views/my_home_page.dart';
 3 import 'package:flutter/material.dart';
 4 import 'package:provider/provider.dart';
 5
 6 void main() {
 7 runApp(
 8 ChangeNotifierProvider(
 9 create: (context) =>
10 CountingTheNumber(),
11 child: MyApp(),
12 ),
13 );
14 }
```

```
15
16 class MyApp extends StatelessWidget {
17 // This widget is the root of your application.
18 @override
19 Widget build(BuildContext context) {
20 return MaterialApp(
21 title: 'Flutter Demo',
22 theme: ThemeData(
23 primarySwatch: Colors.blue,
24 ),
25 home: MyHomePage(),
26 );
27 }
28 }
```

It creates a context that returns the model from where the data comes. And it also returns a child widget, which will consume the data.

For more Flutter related Articles and Resources

Why we need a Model?

For a simple reason. First of all it will store and give us changed data. Although in this example the data is ephemeral, or short-lived, still we need a small model class.

```
1 import 'package:flutter/widgets.dart';
2
3 class CountingTheNumber with ChangeNotifier {
4 int number = 0;
5 void increaseNumber() {
6 number++;
7 notifyListeners();
8 }
9 }
```

Now we can provide this designed model to the desired widget. However our desired widget positions itself at the lowest-bottom.

```
 1 import
'package:basic_flutter_provider/controllers/a_very_deep_widget_tree.dar
t';
 2
 3 import 'package:flutter/material.dart';
 4
 5 class MyHomePage extends StatelessWidget {
 6 @override
 7 Widget build(BuildContext context) {
 8 return Scaffold(
 9 appBar: AppBar(
10 title: Text('Basic Provider Explained to Beginners'),
11 ),
```

```
12 body: Center(
13 child: AVeryDeepWidgetTree(),
14 // This trailing comma makes auto-formatting nicer for build
methods.
15 ));
16 }
17 }
```

While sending our data directly to the lowest-bottom we shouldn't rebuild the top-widgets.

AVeryDeepWidgetTree class is a long code snippet. However you can study the code structure better in my GitHub repo.

Let us see how it works. I will explain what is happening exactly inside. A Very Deep and Nested Widget Tree

As I have said earlier, Flutter allows nested widget tree. In fact, you cannot imagine a complex app without that.

Let us see the code first. Then I'll explain what is happening.

```
1       import
'package:basic_flutter_provider/models/counting_the_number.dart';
2       import 'package:flutter/material.dart';
3       import 'package:provider/provider.dart';
4
5       class AVeryDeepWidgetTree extends StatelessWidget {
6       @override
7       Widget build(BuildContext context) {
8       // 'Provider.of', just like Consumer needs to know the type of
the model.
9       //We need to specify the model 'CountingTheNumber'.
10      final counter = Provider.of<CountingTheNumber>(context);
11      return Container(
12      padding: const EdgeInsets.all(20.0),
13      child: Column(
14      mainAxisAlignment: MainAxisAlignment.center,
15      children: <Widget>[
16      Text(
17      'This is a simple Text widget',
18      style: TextStyle(
19      color: Colors.black,
20      fontSize: 45.0,
21      fontWeight: FontWeight.bold,
22      ),
23      ),
24      //now we are going to build a very deep widget tree
25      Center(
26      child: Container(
27      child: Column(
```

```dart
28      mainAxisAlignment: MainAxisAlignment.center,
29      children: [
30      Text(
31      'This is another simple Text widget deep inside the tree.',
32      style: TextStyle(
33      fontSize: 35.0,
34      fontWeight: FontWeight.bold,
35      ),
36      ),
37      SizedBox(
38      height: 5.0,
39      ),
40      Text(
41      'You have pushed the button this many times:',
42      style: TextStyle(fontSize: 35.0),
43      ),
44      SizedBox(
45      height: 5.0,
46      ),
47      Text(
48      '${counter.number}',
49      style: TextStyle(fontSize: 25.0),
50      ),
51      SizedBox(
52      height: 5.0,
53      ),
54      FloatingActionButton(
55      onPressed: () {
56      counter.increaseNumber();
57      },
58      tooltip: 'Increment',
59      child: Icon(Icons.add),
60      ),
61      ],
62      ),
63      ),
64      ),
65      ],
66      ),
67      );
68      }
69      }
```

Remember our model class. We have only one variable that will reflect the state change. So at the bottom-most widget we need to access it.

To do that, we will use Provider.of() method. Where we should mention the type of our model, and pass the context.

```dart
1 final counter = Provider.of<CountingTheNumber>(context);
```

The Provider helps us to access the model data and method anywhere inside that widget tree.

```
 1 Text(
 2 '${counter.number}',
 3 style: TextStyle(fontSize: 25.0),
 4 ),
 5 SizedBox(
 6 height: 5.0,
 7 ),
 8 FloatingActionButton(
 9 onPressed: () {
10 counter.increaseNumber();
11 },
12 tooltip: 'Increment',
13 child: Icon(Icons.add),
14 ),
```

Clicking the button will change the state of the app by increasing the number.

The main drawback of the above code hides itself in this line of Code:

```
1 final CountingTheNumber counter =
Provider.of<CountingTheNumber>(context);
```

We want to rebuild only the text part where the number will show itself. And we want to rebuild the floating action button section.

Achieving that is easy. All we need to write a separate widget for those parts. After that we will call it inside our view.

```
 1 import 'package:flutter/material.dart';
 2 import
'package:flutter_provider_explained_for_beginners/model/counting_the_nu
mber.d\
 3 art';
 4 import 'package:provider/provider.dart';
 5
 6 class ColumnClass extends StatelessWidget {
 7 @override
 8 Widget build(BuildContext context) {
 9 // 'Provider.of', just like Consumer needs to know the type of the
model.
10 // We need to specify the model 'CountingTheNumber'.
11 //this time only this widget will be rebuilt
12 final CountingTheNumber counter =
Provider.of<CountingTheNumber>(context);
13 return Column(
14 children: [
15 Text(
16 '${counter.number}',
```

```
17 style: TextStyle(fontSize: 25.0),
18 ),
19 SizedBox(height: 10.0),
20 FloatingActionButton(
21 onPressed: () {
22 counter.increaseNumber();
23 },
24 tooltip: 'Increment',
25 child: Icon(Icons.add),
26 )
27 ],
28 );
29 }
30 }
```

Next, we will add this widget to the "AVeryDeepWidgetTree":

```
1 // the whole top widgets will remain unaffected when state changes
2 ColumnClass(),
```

That's all. Running the code will only change a very small segment when we press the button and change the state.

We have successfully removed the pitfalls of rebuilding the whole widget tree. What is flutter provider? How does provider flutter work?

The change of state affects a small segment of widget.

For more Flutter related Articles and Resources

9 . How do you use Provider Consumer to manage State in Flutter?

How do you use provider Consumer widget to manage state? Is it better than Provider.of()<T> to manage state?

Well, let us check that. Here is a simple guide.

We have seen what is Flutter state before. Although I've not written on state management in flutter alone, but I have written on provider before.In that article I've written on how to manage state in Flutter.

I've also written on the relationship between flutter InheritedWidget and State.

However, I've not written on how to use provider Consumer widget. So in this article I'll show it.

How do you use provider consumer to manage state? Very simple.

If you've already have read the previous article on Provider,of() method, and understood the concept, you can use consumer quite easily. What is better? Provider.of<T> or Consumer<T>?

The author of Provider package Rémi Rousselet in an answer mentioned a few key points.

Consumer allows us to build more granular widgets. At the same time, it also solves most BuildContext misuse.

In a minute we will learn how we can take those advantages.

Rémi Rousselet also said that the choice is yours. So you can use any one of them. Although you can use any one of them, without context your preference is meaningless nevertheless.

Keeping context in my mind, I'll always prefer using Consumer<T>, instead of Provider.of()<T>.

Why? I am going to show you in a minute. What is the best state management architecture in Flutter?

I opened the Flutter documentation page on 25th December, 2020 and found this line:

** If you are new to Flutter and you don't have a strong reason to choose another approach (Redux, Rx, hooks, etc.), this is probably the approach you should start with. The provider package is easy to understand and it doesn't use much code. It also uses concepts that are applicable in every other approach. **

As a big admirer of Provider package, I also recommend my readers to use provider. From the very beginning. Provider manages state in the simplest way.

Although, you can use a bit low-level InheritedWidget concept, still that has some limitations. I mentioned that in my previous chapter. You can pass data and services to the descendant widgets by using InheritedWidget concept.

But Provider makes it more simple. In fact, provider actually works with these low-level widgets.

For more Flutter related Articles and Resources

How do you use Provider Consumer?

First add the provider package in your pubspecy.yaml file. Next, you need to import that package.

```
1 import 'package:provider/provider.dart';
```

We will import other packages if needed.

The main problem lies in widget rebuilding process.

We don't want that. Flutter's default State object rebuilds the whole widget tree. While managing state in the deepest widget, we cannot allow this to happen.

Suppose at the bottom of widget tree, inside any Text widget we want to reflect our state change.

To do that, we cannot allow the top widgets to rebuild themselves. What is the solution?

The solution is Provider and Consumer. It starts with ChangeNotifierProvider.

ChangeNotifierProvider is the widget that provides an instance of a ChangeNotifier to its descendants. It comes from the provider package.

We should keep it at the topmost place of our widget tree. Why should we do this?

Let us try to understand the mechanism of state management in Flutter, first. Flutter is a declarative framework. If we want to change the state of UI, we should rebuild it.

Suppose we want to change the bottom-most widget. We cannot do that imperatively from outside, by calling a method on it.

Is there any way so that we can let Flutter help us?

Yes, there is.

We don't want to fight with it, or force it to adopt something that goes against its nature. On the contrary, we will take help from Flutter to do that heavy lifting.

How Flutter helps us to manage State?

ChangeNotifier class provides notification to its listeners. You will find this class in Flutter Software Development Kit (SDK).

In the Provider package, ChangeNotifier is one way to encapsulate the state.

Have a look at our model class.

```
 1 import 'package:flutter/widgets.dart';
 2
 3 class CountingTheNumber with ChangeNotifier {
 4 int number = 0;
 5 String message = 'Sanjib Sinha';
 6
 7 void increaseNumber(int number) {
 8 number++;
 9 notifyListeners();
10 }
```

```
11
12 void testMessage() {
13 message.startsWith('S')
14 ? message = 'Hi Sanjib'
15 : message = 'First letter is not S';
16 notifyListeners();
17 }
18 }
```

The only code that is specific to ChangeNotifier is the call to notifyListeners(). We have called it twice in our methods. (See the code above).

How could we notify Listeners?

We need ChangeNotifierProvider widget that provides an instance of a ChangeNotifier to its descendants. It comes from the provider package.

Now our task becomes much easier. Because we place ChangeNotifierProvider at the top of the all widgets, any descendant widget can access state from it directly.

```
 1 import 'package:flutter/material.dart';
 2 import
'package:flutter_provider_explained_for_beginners/model/counting_the_nu
mber.d\
 3 art';
 4 import
'package:flutter_provider_explained_for_beginners/view/my_home_page.dar
t';
 5 import 'package:provider/provider.dart';
 6
 7 void main() {
 8 runApp(
 9 // ChangeNotifierProvider, unlike ChangeNotifier, comes from the
Provider package
10 // and it provides an instance of a ChangeNotifier to the widgets,
11 // which have already subscribed to it
12 // we should place the ChangeNotifierProvider Just above the widgets
that need to ac\
13 cess it.
14 // you will understand provider better if you already have
understood how
15 // InheritedWidget works
16 ChangeNotifierProvider(
17 create: (context) =>
18 CountingTheNumber(), // designed Model is provided to the desired
widgets
19 child: MyApp(),
20 ),
21 );
22 }
```

```
23
24 class MyApp extends StatelessWidget {
25 // This widget is the root of your application.
26 @override
27 Widget build(BuildContext context) {
28 return MaterialApp(
29 title: 'Flutter Demo',
30 theme: ThemeData(
31 primarySwatch: Colors.blue,
32 ),
33 home: MyHomePage(),
34 );
35 }
36 }
```

Now we can provide CountingTheNumber model to any descendant widgets in our app through the ChangeNotifierProvider. We have declared it already at the top, we can start using it. (See the bold sections at the above and below code).

How we can access changed data? How we can change state through Consumer widget?

We're closing towards the lesser known facts to the unknown world of provider package. As we have just seen the ChangeNotifierProvider provides only one class here. The CountingTheNumber model class, which we have placed in our models folder.

Next, we'll try to solve the next part of the problem.

Where to place the Consumer<T>?

Once our ChangeNotifierProvider provides the CountingTheNumber model class, we can start using it through the Consumer widget.

It is the best practice to put the Consumer widgets as deep as in the tree as possible. That is what we have done.

In our controllers folder, we have created a ColumnClass custom widget that returns a Column widget. In its children section we have two Container widgets, which have the Consumer widgets.

The next code snippet gives you an idea how we use Consumer widget to get the provided model class methods.

```
1 import 'package:flutter/material.dart';
2 import
'package:flutter_provider_explained_for_beginners/model/counting_the_nu
mber.d\
3 art';
4 import 'package:provider/provider.dart';
5
```

```dart
 6 class ColumnClass extends StatelessWidget {
 7 @override
 8 Widget build(BuildContext context) {
 9
10 /// we're using Consumer widget instead of Provider.of().
11 /// we've put our Consumer widget as deep as possible in the tree
12 return Column(
13 children: [
14 Container(
15 margin: const EdgeInsets.all(
16 5.0,
17 ),
18 child: Consumer<CountingTheNumber>(
19 builder: (context, message, child) {
20 return Column(
21 children: [
22 child,
23 Text(
24 '${message.message}',
25 style: TextStyle(fontSize: 25.0),
26 ),
27 ],
28 );
29 },
30
31 /// building a humongous widget tree
32 child: Row(
33 mainAxisAlignment: MainAxisAlignment.center,
34 children: [
35 Column(
36 children: [
37 Text(
38 'First Row',
39 style: TextStyle(
40 fontSize: 20.0,
41 color: Colors.blue,
42 ),
43 ),
44 SizedBox(
45 height: 10.0,
46 ),
47 Text(
48 'Second Row',
49 style: TextStyle(
50 fontSize: 20.0,
51 color: Colors.red,
52 ),
53 ),
54 ],
55 ),
```

```dart
56 const Divider(
57 color: Colors.black,
58 height: 20,
59 thickness: 5,
60 indent: 20,
61 endIndent: 0,
62 ),
63 Column(
64 children: [
65 Text(
66 'First Row',
67 style: TextStyle(
68 fontSize: 20.0,
69 color: Colors.red,
70 ),
71 ),
72 SizedBox(
73 height: 10.0,
74 ),
75 Text(
76 'Second Row',
77 style: TextStyle(
78 fontSize: 20.0,
79 color: Colors.blue,
80 ),
81 ),
82 ],
83 ),
84 ],
85 ),
86 ),
87 ),
88 SizedBox(height: 10.0),
89 Container(
90 margin: const EdgeInsets.all(
91 5.0,
92 ),
93 child: Consumer<CountingTheNumber>(
94 builder: (context, message, child) {
95 return Column(
96 children: [
97 FloatingActionButton(
98 onPressed: () {
99 message.testMessage();
100 },
101 tooltip: 'Increment',
102 child: Icon(Icons.ac_unit_rounded),
103 ),
104 child,
105 ],
```

```
106 );
107 },
108
109 /// building another humongous widget tree
110 child: Row(
111 mainAxisAlignment: MainAxisAlignment.center,
112 children: [
113 Column(
114 children: [
115 Text(
116 'First Row',
117 style: TextStyle(
118 fontSize: 20.0,
119 color: Colors.blue,
120 ),
121 ),
122 SizedBox(
123 height: 10.0,
124 ),
125 Text(
126 'Second Row',
127 style: TextStyle(
128 fontSize: 20.0,
129 color: Colors.red,
130 ),
131 ),
132 ],
133 ),
134 const Divider(
135 color: Colors.black,
136 height: 20,
137 thickness: 5,
138 indent: 20,
139 endIndent: 0,
140 ),
141 Column(
142 children: [
143 Text(
144 'First Row',
145 style: TextStyle(
146 fontSize: 20.0,
147 color: Colors.red,
148 ),
149 ),
150 SizedBox(
151 height: 10.0,
152 ),
153 Text(
154 'Second Row',
155 style: TextStyle(
```

```
156 fontSize: 20.0,
157 color: Colors.blue,
158 ),
159 ),
160 ],
161 ),
162 ],
163 ),
164 ),
165 ),
166 ],
167 );
168 }
169 }
```

Watch the bold sections. Reading them will explain how Consumer widgets work. How do the Consumer widgets work?

The bold sections in the above code tells us one thing. In a Consumer widget we must specify the type of the model that we want to access.

```
1 child: Consumer<CountingTheNumber>()
```

Here the model class is CountingTheNumber() that has two methods. When we call one method that increases the number of the counter variable.

We have seen its usage in our previous article, where we have used Provide.of()<T>.

The another method of the model class helps us to search and find one character. By pressing the button we check whether the message starts with that letter or not.

Clicking the button changes the state of the associated widget and gives us a message.

When we click the blue icon button, it calls the method on our model class that checks whether the name has started with letter 's' or not. If it starts with that letter it gives a welcome message.

Now everything happens without rebuilding the whole widget tree. Take a good look at my GitHub repo : The Flutter Provider code repository for this book

You will find how we have built a humongous widget tree above and below of our Consumer widgets.

The Specific Steps to use Consumer widget

We should know each individual steps that we exercise to use Consumer widgets.

The very first step involves specifying the type of the model class. We have already seen that line in the above code.

```
1 Consumer<CountingTheNumber>
```

What happens if we don't specify the generics? The provider package cannot help us any more. The provider is based on types. If you don't mention the type, it doesn't know what to provide.

The only required argument of Consumer widget is builder. Understanding how the builder function works, is very important.

Each time we try to change the state by pressing the button, the ChangeNotifier changes. In fact, we call the notifyListeners() in our model class methods, just like below:

```
1 void testMessage() {
2 message.startsWith('S')
3 ? message = 'Hi Sanjib'
4 : message = 'First letter is not S';
5 notifyListeners();
6 }
```

Consequently it calls all the builder methods of all the corresponding Consumer widgets. Now the builder method is called with three arguments.

```
1 builder: (context, message, child){}
```

The first argument in any builder function is context. We get context in every build method. The role of context is extremely important, not only in Flutter, but in any language too. A detailed discussion on context is what I'm planning to write. You will get that in Flutter section.

The second argument is the instance of the ChangeNotifier. Here it is message. For this data alone we're using the Consumer widget. Isn't it?

The third argument is child. If you plan to add large sub-tree under the control of your Consumer widget, then just go ahead. Use that child to build more complex UI. However, when state changes, the child does not get affected.

The large sub-tree you've just added under Consumer doesn't change when the model changes.

If you run the code, the first screen shows you a name: "Sanjib Sinha" at the bottom most Widget.

Next, we've pressed the button and it changes the state of the bottom-most Widget, and gives us a message, such as "Hi Sanjib". While changing the State of the bottom-most Widget, it does not change the top and bottom widgets.

So, that's it. Although I feel we should learn provider using more complex examples.

We'll learn Provider by building more complex UI in the coming chapters.

For more Flutter related Articles and Resources

10. How do you use onPressed in flutter?

Whenever we think of Flutter, two things come to our mind. One is Widget, and the other is UI.

The Flutter framework helps us to build beautiful design patterns. If you have already known Flutter a little bit, then you must have learned one key concept.

You cannot drag and drop interfaces. Instead you need to write the necessary code.

However, since the coding part involves only Dart programming language, it becomes easier for you. Of course, you should have a basic Dart programming concept.

Now, in this context, we come to the second point. Any User Interface needs user's interaction. Your Flutter app should allow users to interact with itself. No matter, how you design that app.

As long as we think of UI and interaction, we can think of a simple button. If we press that button, it should call a method in your widget class.

Think about the RaisedButton widget that uses a callback through onPressed.

In this article we would like to understand this key concept of onPressed in Flutter.

For more Flutter related Articles and Resources

How do you use onPressed in flutter?

To understand onPressed, we need to use it inside a Flutter app, first. Let's go step by step.

First we should import material and call our main OurApp class using void main runApp method.

```
1 import 'package:flutter/material.dart';
2
3 void main() {
4 runApp(OurApp());
5 }
```

Our next job involves creating a class named as OurApp that extends StatelessWidget and it should have a build() method.

```
1 class OurApp extends StatelessWidget {
2 @override
3 Widget build(BuildContext context) {
4 return MaterialApp(
5 title: 'Our App',
6 debugShowCheckedModeBanner: false,
```

```dart
 7 home: Scaffold(
 8 body: ACenterClass(),
 9 ),
10 );
11 }
12 }
13
14 class ACenterClass extends StatelessWidget {
15 void pressRemote() {
16 print('Remote has been pressed.');
17 }
18
19 @override
20 Widget build(BuildContext context) {
21 return Center(
22 child: Container(
23 alignment: Alignment.center,
24 width: 350.00,
25 height: 350.00,
26 decoration: BoxDecoration(
27 color: Colors.blue,
28 border: Border.all(
29 color: Colors.deepOrange,
30 width: 2.0,
31 style: BorderStyle.solid,
32 ),
33 borderRadius: BorderRadius.all(Radius.circular(40.0)),
34 boxShadow: [
35 BoxShadow(
36 color: Colors.black54,
37 blurRadius: 20.0,
38 spreadRadius: 20.0,
39 ),
40 ],
41 gradient: LinearGradient(
42 begin: Alignment.centerLeft,
43 end: Alignment.centerRight,
44 colors: [
45 Colors.red,
46 Colors.white,
47 ],
48 ),
49 // to make shape active we need to comment out borderRadius property
and vice versa
50 //shape: BoxShape.circle,
51 ),
52 child: Column(
53 children: [
54 Text(
55 'Press',
```

```
56 style: TextStyle(
57 fontSize: 30.0,
58 color: Colors.blue,
59 ),
60 ),
61 SizedBox(
62 height: 10.0,
63 ),
64 RaisedButton(
65 child: Text(
66 'Press Button',
67 style: TextStyle(
68 fontSize: 30.0,
69 color: Colors.blue,
70 ),
71 ),
72 onPressed: pressRemote,
73 ),
74 ],
75 ),
76 ),
77 );
78 }
79 }
```

As you see in the above code, we have called a function pressRemote(), or we should call it a method since it is inside a class.

How do you call a function in flutter?

How did we call a function in Flutter? We have also created a standalone Class named as ACenterClass that extends StatelessWidget.

Inside ACenterClass, we have created a function pressRemote() that simply prints a message when user presses the RaisedButton.

```
1 void pressRemote() {
2 print('Remote has been pressed.');
3 }
4
5 ...
6
7 RaisedButton(
8 child: Text(
9 'Press Button',
10 style: TextStyle(
11 fontSize: 30.0,
12 color: Colors.blue,
13 ),
14 ),
```

```
15 onPressed: pressRemote,
16 ),
```

As we press the button, it debugs and prints the message in our terminal – Remote has been pressed.

However, there is a question.

Inside RaisedButton Widget onPressed callback we have passed a reference of the function pressRemote(). See the code below:

```
1 onPressed: pressRemote,
```

We cannot write like this:

```
1 onPressed: pressRemote(),
```

But, why?

To understand onPressed, you need to understand a key concept of Dart programming language.

What is flutter function?

A function, also we might reference to as method in the context of an object, is a block of code that is nothing but a subset of algorithm separated logically, and we can reuse it.

Now a function can return nothing (void) or return either a built-in data type or a custom data type.

It can also have no parameters or any number of parameters.

Now, RaisedButton widget through its constructor uses onPressed as a callback function.

What is callback in flutter?

The Callback is a function or a method which we pass as an argument into another function or method.

Exactly that happens here. We have passed onPressed as a named argument into RaisedButton constructor.

And what happens after that?

The onPressed performs an action. It uses callback concept.

Let us see almost similar code snippet in Dart, so it clears up everything.

```
1 class PressButton {
2 bool pressOn = true;
3 bool pressButton(bool pressOn) {
```

```
 4 if (pressOn) {
 5 return true;
 6 } else {
 7 return false;
 8 }
 9 }
10 }
11
12 class Remote {
13 Remote({bool onPress});
14 void remoteOn(Function({bool onPress}) Remote) {
15 print('Tv is on.');
16 }
17 }
18
19 void main(List<String> args) {
20 var button = PressButton();
21 var tvIsOn = button.pressButton(true);
22 var remote = Remote(onPress: tvIsOn);
23 remote.remoteOn(({onPress}) => tvIsOn);
24 }
25
26 /// the output is like the following
27 /// TV is on
```

We have referenced the function and it returns the value.

For more Flutter related Articles and Resources

11. Provider: A recommended approach to manage State

When an app is running, sometimes we want something, such as user's log-in session or added item in the cart, to exist in memory.

If we want something to exist in memory, we can call it 'state'.

In the previous chapters, we have already discussed 'state' in various lavels.

We have also learned a few tricks to manage it.

However, that is an introduction. We need to understand the concept of 'state', because it is extremely important to build any type of complex app, that handles multiple screens, different variables, user sessions, etc.

State can include anything – the app's assets, as we said, all the variables that the Flutter framework keeps about the UI, user sessions that can be shared in different parts of the app, etc.

Whenever we design an app, and start building it, we don't have to manage every state.

Flutter framework takes care of a large sections, like textures. Despite that,we need some data to rebuild our UI at any moment in time.

The simplest example is we press a button and the text changes on the screen.

Again we press the restore button, and the text disappears. We need to provide the business logic so that it happens.

Consider a complex example, where a user adds an item to cart and that item remains at that cart as long as user is logged in.

Now, state is of two types – ephemeral and app state.

We know the meaning of the word ephemeral, it means short-lived. Some kind of state is very short-lived.

We may contain it in a single widget. That is why it is also called local state. Suppose we want to show the current progress of a complex animation. Once it is done, the UI is rebuilt, and we don't want it anymore.

For that reason, we don't have to need any specialized state management techniques like 'Provider' for that.

Let us see an example of ephemeral state or short-lived state. Suppose we have a list of questions and answers. User can press the button and change to the next question.

The app is quite straight forward and simple. To start with we need to organize our application in three directories - controller, model and view.

The main.dart file and the main method calls the runApp() method, in which we pass our app - QuizApp().

```
1 import 'package:flutter/material.dart';
2 import 'package:quiz_app/view/quiz_app.dart';
3
4 void main() {
5 runApp(QuizApp());
6 }
```

Next we need quiz_app.dart file in view directory.

```
1 import 'package:flutter/material.dart';
2 import 'package:quiz_app/view/home_page.dart';
3
4 class QuizApp extends StatelessWidget {
5 // This widget is the root of your application.
6 @override
7 Widget build(BuildContext context) {
```

```
 8      return MaterialApp(
 9      title: 'Flutter Demo',
10      theme: ThemeData(
11          primarySwatch: Colors.blue,
12      ),
13      home: MyHomePage(title: 'Quiz App Home Page'),
14      );
15 }
16 }
```

The MaterialApp Widget again returns MyHomePage() and we will get that in view directory.

By the way, it will be a stateful widget.

```
 1 import 'package:flutter/material.dart';
 2 import 'package:quiz_app/controller/question_widget.dart';
 3 import 'package:quiz_app/model/questions_list.dart';
 4
 5 class MyHomePage extends StatefulWidget {
 6 MyHomePage({Key key, this.title}) : super(key: key);
 7
 8 final String title;
 9
10 @override
11 _MyHomePageState createState() => _MyHomePageState();
12 }
13
14 class _MyHomePageState extends State<MyHomePage> {
15 int _counter = 0;
16
17 void _incrementCounter() {
18     setState(() {
19     _counter++;
20     });
21     if (_counter > 2) {
22     _counter = 0;
23     }
24 }
25
26 @override
27 Widget build(BuildContext context) {
28     var questions = questionList;
29     return Scaffold(
30     appBar: AppBar(
31         title: Text(widget.title),
32     ),
33     body: Center(
34         child: Column(
35         mainAxisAlignment: MainAxisAlignment.center,
```

```
36          children: <Widget>[
37              QuestionWidget(questions: questions, counter: _counter),
38              ...(questions[_counter]['answers'] as List<String>)
39                  .map(
40                  (answer) => buildElevatedButton(answer),
41                  )
42                  .toList(),
43          ],
44          ),
45      ),
46      // This trailing comma makes auto-formatting nicer for build
methods.
47      );
48 }
49
50 ElevatedButton buildElevatedButton(String answer) {
51      return ElevatedButton(
52      onPressed: _incrementCounter,
53      child: Text(
54          answer,
55          style: TextStyle(
56          fontSize: 30.0,
57          ),
58      ),
59      );
60 }
61 }
```

As you have noticed, we need two more files. One stays in model directory. It consists of a List of questions and different answers.

Basically, it is a List of Map that consists of two data types, String as key and Object or List as value.

```
1 List<Map<String, Object>> questionList = [
2 {
3      'question': 'What is the synonym of Mendacity?',
4      'answers': ['truthfulness', 'daring', 'falsehood', 'enemy'],
5 },
6 {
7      'question': 'What is the synonym of Culpable?',
8      'answers': ['gay', 'guilty', 'falsehood', 'enemy'],
9 },
10 {
11      'question': 'What is the synonym of Rapacious?',
12      'answers': ['guilty', 'daring', 'falsehood', 'greedy'],
13 },
14 ];
```

Finally we go to the controller directory and fetch the Question widget.

```dart
1  import 'package:flutter/material.dart';
2
3  class QuestionWidget extends StatelessWidget {
4  const QuestionWidget({
5      Key key,
6      @required this.questions,
7      @required int counter,
8  })  : _counter = counter,
9          super(key: key);
10
11 final List<Map<String, Object>> questions;
12 final int _counter;
13
14 @override
15 Widget build(BuildContext context) {
16     return Text(
17     questions[_counter]['question'],
18     style: TextStyle(
19         fontSize: 25.0,
20         fontWeight: FontWeight.bold,
21     ),
22     );
23 }
24 }
```

Nothing fancy althogh, it gives us an idea of how we can organize our small ephemeral state in a single widget.

For more Flutter related Articles and Resources

Ephemeral State or Single Widget is not enough

As our application grows and we need different screens or views, many widgets, we the single widget approach to manage ephemeral state is not enough.

There are many other techniques as well, but in this chapter we will only learn Provider, because Google recommends it.

For ephemeral state management using setState() and a field inside the StatefulWidget's State class is enough, because, a single widget needs it, no other part of the device can access its single private variable.

An app state or application state is not like that. We want to share the app state across many parts of our app, not only that, we may want it to keep between user sessions. In like manner, we can call it shared state.

To manage app state we can opt for several options. Nevertheless, Google recommends Provider, we will have a brief look at other options as well.

As we have said before, Provider is the recommended approach. Provider helps you to manage state efficiently, in a very simple and it has great flexibility.

We will learn that techniques in a minute.

Before that, let us see other approaches to manage state. Using setState() and a field inside the StatefulWidget's State class is another approach; yet that is good and recommended for the ephemeral state. This lower-level approach is made up when we create a new Flutter application.

InheritedWidget & InheritedModel approach is another lower-level approach that communicates between ancestors and children in the widget tree. We have seen how we can manage state through Inherited Widget in our previous chapter.

Redux is another approach that is familiar to the web developers. It is a state container approach, which is also very popular among Flutter developers.

BLoC is another stream and observable based patterns, in fact before Provider has stepped in, BLoC was very popular. Still the flutter community adores BLoC.

Otherwise we might use MobX or GetX approach; the first one is a popular library based conceptualization on observables and reactions, and the second one is a simplified reactive state management solution.

There are plenty of open source resources available to learn any one of them, thoroughly.

In this chapter, although, we will learn only Provider, the state management recommended by Google, creator of Dart programming language and Flutter framework.

A Step by Step guide to use Provider

First thing first, we have add the dependency on provider to our 'pubspec.yaml' file.

```
1 // pubspec.yaml
2 # ...
3
4 dependencies:
5 flutter:
6     sdk: flutter
7
8 provider: ^4.0.0
```

At the time of writing this book, provider package is 4 and above. We will always check the latest version.

The app state is something that we need to modify from many different places, and to do that we have to pass around a lot of callbacks; for a complex widget tree, it will be suicidal to replace several widgets again and again.

To understand this mechanism we need to find out a solution that will not disturb the widget tree as a whole, yet the app state will modify a few widgets deep down the tree. Suppose we need to modify one widget that has hundred widgets on top of it.

Without disturbing top hundred widgets, we can successfully handle the app state using Provider.

Flutter has in-built mechanisms for widgets to provide data and services to their distant descendants, it means not just the immediate children, but any widgets below them.

Provider makes it possible to forget the callbacks and InheritedWidgets. We need to understand three primary concepts:

```
1 ChangeNotifier
2 ChangeNotifierProvider
3 Consumer
```

ChangeNotifier is an in-built class included in the Flutter SDK, this class notifies the listeners when any change in the state of the ChangeNotifier class takes place. Any widget having hundreds widgets on the top, can subscribe to its changes.

ChangeNotifierProvider, unlike ChangeNotifier, comes from the Provider package and it provides an instance of a ChangeNotifier to the widgets, which have already subscribed to it.

Where we should place the ChangeNotifierProvider? Just above the widgets that need to access it.

```
1 void main() {
2 runApp(
3     ChangeNotifierProvider(
4     create: (context) => AnyModel(),
5     child: HomeApp(),
6     ),
7 );
8 }
```

Or we can even use MultiProvider, if we want to use multiple classes.

```
1 void main() {
2 runApp(
3     MultiProvider(
4     providers: [
5         ChangeNotifierProvider(create: (context) => FirstModel()),
6         Provider(create: (context) => SecondClass()),
```

```
 7      ],
 8      child: HomeApp(),
 9      ),
10  );
11  }
```

Once our designed Model is provided to the desired widgets in our app through the ChangeNotifierProvider declaration at the top, the Consumer widgets that have subscribed to the notifications can use it.

```
1 return Consumer<FirstModel>(
2 builder: (context, value, child) {
3      return Text("The value : ${value.firstModelVariable}");
4 },
5 );
```

The first rule of using Consumer widget is we need to be specific about the type of the model that we want to access. Suppose, we want 'FirstModel', so we write Consumer<FirstModel>.

If the generic type <FirstModel> is not specified, the Provider package cannot help us.

** The Provider package is based on 'type'. Therefore, we must mention the type. **

The second most important rule is we must supply the 'builder' argument of the Consumer widget. This is the only required argument of the Consumer widget.

Whenever in the model class ChangeNotifier changes, the builder argument is called.

Let us try to understand what is happening. Whenever the ChangeNotifier changes, the method notifyListeners() is called, and at the same time, all the builder methods of all the corresponding Consumer widgets are called.

The 'builder' is called with three arguments, the first one is quite familiar,'context'; we get it in every build method. The second argument 'value' is the instance of the ChangeNotifier. Using that instance we can define the app state, and along with it, we can also use the data in the model according to our requirement.

The role of the third argument 'child' is quite interesting. Suppose we have a large widget subtree under our Consumer that does not change when our model changes.

We can also get it through the builder argument 'child'.

We have done enough talking, tried to understand the interaction between Provider, and Consumer. Nonetheless, we won't understand this concepts unless we try to implement them.

Let us start with a very simple counter model. Through Provider, we will change the counter number. We have two buttons – Increase and Decrease (Figure 8.1).

Imagine a number line, using these buttons, we can either move towards the right side (positive), or towards the left side (negative).

Figure 11.1 – Simple Provider example

The next two images will show you how we have increased the value and decreased the value tapping these two buttons respectively.

But before that we need to see the code and try to understand how we have used the Provider package.

```
1 import 'package:flutter/widgets.dart';
2
3 /// using the mixin concept of dart that we have discussed
4 /// in our previous chapter
5 class CountingTheNumber with ChangeNotifier {
6 int value = 0;
7 void incrementTheValue() {
8     value++;
9     notifyListeners();
10 }
11
12 void decreaseValue() {
13     value--;
14     notifyListeners();
15 }
16 }
```

The above code snippets is quite simple. This is our model class through which we want to manage the state of the counter in a ChangeNotifier.

Next, we need to use the ChangeNotifierProvider in the right place.

Because we need to call two methods, using Consumer is wasteful. We don't want to change the whole UI with the help of our model data.

That is why we will use another concept - 'Provider.of', instead of using Consumer.

```dart
1 import 'package:flutter/cupertino.dart';
2 import 'package:flutter/material.dart';
3 import 'package:provider/provider.dart';
4
5 import 'counter_class.dart';
6
7 class MyApp extends StatelessWidget {
8 // This widget is the root of your application.
9 @override
10 Widget build(BuildContext context) {
11     return MaterialApp(
12     title: 'Flutter Demo',
13     theme: ThemeData(
14         primarySwatch: Colors.blue,
15         visualDensity: VisualDensity.adaptivePlatformDensity,
16     ),
17     home: ChangeNotifierProvider<CountingTheNumber>(
18         // it will not redraw the whole widget tree anymore
19         create: (BuildContext context) => CountingTheNumber(),
20         child: MyHomePage()),
21     );
22 }
23 }
24
25 class MyHomePage extends StatelessWidget {
26 /*
27 MyHomePage({Key key, this.title}) : super(key: key);
28
29 final String title;
30 */
31
32 @override
33 Widget build(BuildContext context) {
34     final counter = Provider.of<CountingTheNumber>(context);
35     return Scaffold(
36     appBar: AppBar(
37         title: Text('Using Provider Example One'),
38     ),
39     body: Center(
40         child: Column(
41         mainAxisAlignment: MainAxisAlignment.center,
42         children: <Widget>[
43             Text(
44             'You have pushed the button this many times:',
45             ),
```

```
46          // only Text widget listens to the notification
47          Text(
48          '${counter.value}',
49          style: Theme.of(context).textTheme.headline4,
50          ),
51          SizedBox(
52          height: 10.0,
53          ),
54          RaisedButton(
55          onPressed: () => counter.incrementTheValue(),
56          child: Text(
57              'Increase',
58              style: TextStyle(
59              fontSize: 20.0,
60              ),
61          ),
62          ),
63          SizedBox(
64          height: 10.0,
65          ),
66          RaisedButton(
67          onPressed: () => counter.decreaseValue(),
68          child: Text(
69              'Decrease',
70              style: TextStyle(
71              fontSize: 20.0,
72              ),
73          ),
74          ),
75        ],
76        ),
77     ),
78     // This trailing comma makes auto-formatting nicer for build
methods.
79     );
80 }
81 }
```

Now, we can run the app and by tapping two buttons change the value. Before that, let us have a close look at some parts of the above code.

```
1 final counter = Provider.of<CountingTheNumber>(context);
```

'Provider.of', just like Consumer needs to know the type of the model. We need to specify the model 'CountingTheNumber'. Now using the 'counter' we have accessed the model data.

```
1 Text(
2              '${counter.value}',
3              style: Theme.of(context).textTheme.headline4,
```

```
 4              ),
 5 …
 6 RaisedButton(
 7            onPressed: () => counter.incrementTheValue(),
 8            child: Text(
 9                'Increase',
10                style: TextStyle(
11                fontSize: 20.0,
12                ),
13            ),
14            ),
15 …
16 RaisedButton(
17            onPressed: () => counter.decreaseValue(),
18            child: Text(
19                'Decrease',
20                style: TextStyle(
21                fontSize: 20.0,
22                ),
23            ),
24            ),
```

The next step is running the app.

```
1 import 'package:flutter/material.dart';
2 import 'utilities/first_provider_example.dart';
3
4 void main() {
5 runApp(MyApp());
6 }
```

Now we can tap the increase button (Figure 8.2).

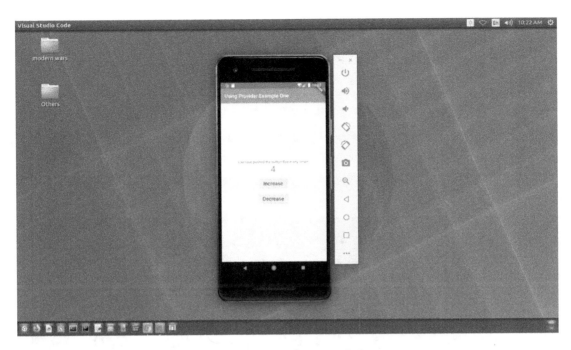

Figure 11.2 – We have tapped the increase button 4 times

After that, we can run the app once again, and it turns the counter value to 0. Now, we can test the decrease button (Figure 8.3).

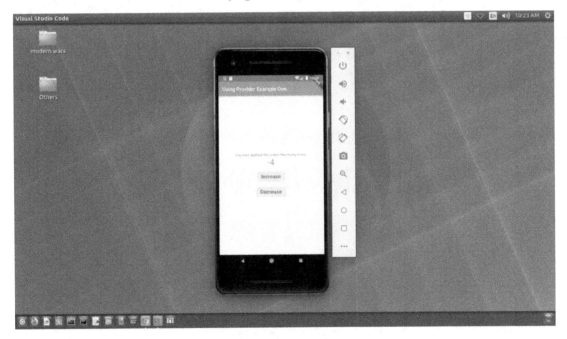

Figure 11.3 – Tapping the decrease button

The above code snippets give us an idea of how Provider package works.

Now we will take closer looks and use multi Providers and multi models to understand this process. This time we will use Consumer.

Let us start with an image. We have extended our old code added a few more generic models.

Now we can press the counter button, and besides, we will press a button to change the text below. After that, we can also press the restore button to clear that data and give an output of that.

Figure 11.4 – Provider example with many models

In the above image, it is evident that we have pressed the decrease button 4 times, however, the default text data - 'Some Data', has not been affected.

Let us see the code:

```
1 //main.dart
2
3 import 'models/providers/first_model_provider.dart';
4
5 import 'models/providers/counter_model_provider.dart';
6 import 'package:flutter/material.dart';
7 import 'package:provider/provider.dart';
8 import 'models/providers/second_model_provider.dart';
9 import 'views/my_app.dart';
10
11 void main() {
12 runApp(MultiProvider(
13     providers: [
```

```dart
14      ChangeNotifierProvider(
15          create: (context) => CountingTheNumber(),
16      ),
17      ChangeNotifierProvider(
18          create: (context) => FirstModelProvider(),
19      ),
20      ],
21      child: MyApp(),
22 ));
23 }
24
25
26 // first_model_provider.dart
27
28 import 'package:flutter/widgets.dart';
29
30 class FirstModelProvider with ChangeNotifier {
31 String someDate = 'Some Date';
32
33 void supplyFirstData() {
34      someDate = 'Data Changed!';
35      print(someDate);
36      notifyListeners();
37 }
38
39 void clearData() {
40      someDate = 'Data Cleared!';
41      print(someDate);
42      notifyListeners();
43 }
44 }
45
46
47 // my_home_page.dart
48
49 import
'package:all_about_flutter_provider/models/providers/first_model_provid
er.dar\
50 t';
51 import
'package:all_about_flutter_provider/models/providers/second_model_provi
der.da\
52 rt';
53 import 'package:flutter/cupertino.dart';
54 import 'package:flutter/material.dart';
55 import 'package:provider/provider.dart';
56
57 import '../models/providers/counter_model_provider.dart';
58
59 class MyHomePage extends StatelessWidget {
```

```dart
60 /*
61 MyHomePage({Key key, this.title}) : super(key: key);
62
63 final String title;
64 */
65 final String title = 'Using Provider Examples';
66
67 @override
68 Widget build(BuildContext context) {
69     /// MyHomePage is rebuilt when counter changes
70     final counter = Provider.of<CountingTheNumber>(context);
71
72     return Scaffold(
73     appBar: AppBar(
74         title: Text(title),
75     ),
76     body: SafeArea(
77         child: ListView(
78         padding: const EdgeInsets.all(10.0),
79         children: <Widget>[
80             Text(
81             'You have pushed the button this many times:',
82             style: TextStyle(fontSize: 25.0),
83             textAlign: TextAlign.center,
84             ),
85
86             /// consumer or selector
87             Text(
88             '${counter.value}',
89             style: Theme.of(context).textTheme.headline4,
90             textAlign: TextAlign.center,
91             ),
92             SizedBox(
93             height: 10.0,
94             ),
95             Row(
96             mainAxisAlignment: MainAxisAlignment.spaceEvenly,
97             children: <Widget>[
98                 RaisedButton(
99                 onPressed: () => counter.increaseValue(),
100                child: Text(
101                    'Increase',
102                    style: TextStyle(
103                    fontSize: 20.0,
104                    ),
105                ),
106                ),
107                SizedBox(
108                height: 10.0,
109                ),
```

```
110             RaisedButton(
111             onPressed: () => counter.decreaseValue(),
112             child: Text(
113                 'Decrease',
114                 style: TextStyle(
115                 fontSize: 20.0,
116                 ),
117             ),
118             ),
119         ],
120         ),
121     SizedBox(
122     height: 10.0,
123     ),
124     Column(
125     mainAxisAlignment: MainAxisAlignment.spaceEvenly,
126     children: <Widget>[
127         Container(
128         padding: const EdgeInsets.all(10.0),
129         color: Colors.red,
130         child: Consumer<FirstModelProvider>(
131             builder: (context, firstModelProvider, child)
=>
132                 RaisedButton(
133             child: Text(
134                 'Press me!',
135                 style: TextStyle(fontSize: 20.0),
136             ),
137             onPressed: () {
138                 firstModelProvider.supplyFirstData();
139             },
140             ),
141         ),
142         ),
143         Container(
144         padding: const EdgeInsets.all(10.0),
145         color: Colors.white30,
146         child: Consumer<FirstModelProvider>(
147             builder: (context, firstModelProvider, child)
=> Text(
148             firstModelProvider.someDate,
149             style: TextStyle(fontSize: 40.0),
150             ),
151         ),
152         ),
153         SizedBox(
154         height: 10.0,
155         ),
156         Container(
157         padding: const EdgeInsets.all(10.0),
```

```
158                    color: Colors.red[200],
159                    child: Consumer<FirstModelProvider>(
160                       builder: (context, firstModelProvider, child)
=>
161                          RaisedButton(
162                       child: Text(
163                          'Reset',
164                          style: TextStyle(fontSize: 20.0),
165                       ),
166                       onPressed: () {
167                          firstModelProvider.clearData();
168                       },
169                       ),
170                    ),
171                    ),
172                ],
173                ),
174             ],
175             ),
176          ),
177
178       /// This trailing comma makes auto-formatting nicer for build
methods.
179          );
180 }
181 }
```

In the above code, we have used two Providers, inside the main() function.

```
1 runApp(MultiProvider(
2     providers: [
3     ChangeNotifierProvider(
4        create: (context) => CountingTheNumber(),
5     ),
6     ChangeNotifierProvider(
7        create: (context) => FirstModelProvider(),
8     ),
9     ],
10     child: MyApp(),
11 ));
```

Along with the 'CountingTheNumber' model, we have used a new 'ChangeNotifier' model - 'FirstModelProvider' class. And finally, inside the 'MyHomePage' widget, we have used the Consumer concepts.

```
1 child: Consumer<FirstModelProvider>(
2                    builder: (context, firstModelProvider, child) =>
3                        RaisedButton(
4                    child: Text(
5                       'Press me!',
```

```
 6                          style: TextStyle(fontSize: 20.0),
 7                        ),
 8                      onPressed: () {
 9                          firstModelProvider.supplyFirstData();
10                      },
11                      ),
12                  ),
```

Because this Consumer's builder argument returns a RaisedButton() widget, we have used the onPressed() argument to call one of model methods. It gives us the next figure (Figure 8.5).

Figure 11.5 – The 'Press me' button has been pressed and the value of the model class has also been changed

If we click the 'Reset' button, the data has been cleared. The following figure (Figure 11.5) shows that display of the screen.

Figure 11.6 – We have pressed the 'Reset' button, and the corresponding value of model class is displayed

Now we are going to add another model class in the next code snippets. It will add another button that will display the first name.

```dart
1  // main.dart
2
3  import 'models/providers/first_model_provider.dart';
4
5  import 'models/providers/counter_model_provider.dart';
6  import 'package:flutter/material.dart';
7  import 'package:provider/provider.dart';
8  import 'models/providers/second_model_provider.dart';
9  import 'views/my_app.dart';
10
11 void main() {
12 runApp(MultiProvider(
13     providers: [
14     ChangeNotifierProvider(
15         create: (context) => CountingTheNumber(),
16     ),
17     ChangeNotifierProvider(
18         create: (context) => FirstModelProvider(),
19     ),
20     ChangeNotifierProvider(
21         create: (context) => SecondModelProvider(),
22     ),
23     ],
24     child: MyApp(),
25 ));
```

```
26 }
27
28
29 // second_model_provider.dart
30
31 import 'package:flutter/widgets.dart';
32
33 class SecondModelProvider with ChangeNotifier {
34 String name = 'Some Name';
35 int age = 0;
36
37 void getFirstName() {
38     name = 'Json';
39     print(name);
40     notifyListeners();
41 }
42 }
43
44
45 // my_home_page.dart
46
47 import
'package:all_about_flutter_provider/models/providers/first_model_provid
er.dar\
48 t';
49 import
'package:all_about_flutter_provider/models/providers/second_model_provi
der.da\
50 rt';
51 import 'package:flutter/cupertino.dart';
52 import 'package:flutter/material.dart';
53 import 'package:provider/provider.dart';
54
55 import '../models/providers/counter_model_provider.dart';
56
57 class MyHomePage extends StatelessWidget {
58 /*
59 MyHomePage({Key key, this.title}) : super(key: key);
60
61 final String title;
62 */
63 final String title = 'Using Provider Examples';
64
65 @override
66 Widget build(BuildContext context) {
67     /// MyHomePage is rebuilt when counter changes
68     final counter = Provider.of<CountingTheNumber>(context);
69
70     return Scaffold(
71     appBar: AppBar(
```

```
72            title: Text(title),
73        ),
74      body: SafeArea(
75          child: ListView(
76          padding: const EdgeInsets.all(10.0),
77          children: <Widget>[
78              Text(
79              'You have pushed the button this many times:',
80              style: TextStyle(fontSize: 25.0),
81              textAlign: TextAlign.center,
82              ),
83
84              /// consumer or selector
85              Text(
86              '${counter.value}',
87              style: Theme.of(context).textTheme.headline4,
88              textAlign: TextAlign.center,
89              ),
90              SizedBox(
91              height: 10.0,
92              ),
93              Row(
94              mainAxisAlignment: MainAxisAlignment.spaceEvenly,
95              children: <Widget>[
96                  RaisedButton(
97                  onPressed: () => counter.increaseValue(),
98                  child: Text(
99                      'Increase',
100                     style: TextStyle(
101                     fontSize: 20.0,
102                     ),
103                 ),
104                 ),
105                 SizedBox(
106                 height: 10.0,
107                 ),
108                 RaisedButton(
109                 onPressed: () => counter.decreaseValue(),
110                 child: Text(
111                     'Decrease',
112                     style: TextStyle(
113                     fontSize: 20.0,
114                     ),
115                 ),
116                 ),
117             ],
118             ),
119             SizedBox(
120             height: 10.0,
121             ),
```

```
122             Column(
123             mainAxisAlignment: MainAxisAlignment.spaceEvenly,
124             children: <Widget>[
125                 Container(
126                 padding: const EdgeInsets.all(10.0),
127                 color: Colors.red,
128                 child: Consumer<FirstModelProvider>(
129                     builder: (context, firstModelProvider, child)
=>
130                         RaisedButton(
131                     child: Text(
132                         'Press me!',
133                         style: TextStyle(fontSize: 20.0),
134                     ),
135                     onPressed: () {
136                         firstModelProvider.supplyFirstData();
137                     },
138                     ),
139                 ),
140                 ),
141                 Container(
142                 padding: const EdgeInsets.all(10.0),
143                 color: Colors.white30,
144                 child: Consumer<FirstModelProvider>(
145                     builder: (context, firstModelProvider, child)
=> Text(
146                         firstModelProvider.someDate,
147                         style: TextStyle(fontSize: 40.0),
148                         ),
149                 ),
150                 ),
151                 SizedBox(
152                 height: 10.0,
153                 ),
154                 Container(
155                 padding: const EdgeInsets.all(10.0),
156                 color: Colors.red[200],
157                 child: Consumer<FirstModelProvider>(
158                     builder: (context, firstModelProvider, child)
=>
159                         RaisedButton(
160                     child: Text(
161                         'Reset',
162                         style: TextStyle(fontSize: 20.0),
163                     ),
164                     onPressed: () {
165                         firstModelProvider.clearData();
166                     },
167                     ),
168                 ),
```

```
169                     ),
170                     SizedBox(
171                     height: 10.0,
172                     ),
173                     Container(
174                     padding: const EdgeInsets.all(10.0),
175                     color: Colors.white30,
176                     child: Consumer<SecondModelProvider>(
177                         builder: (context, secondModel, child) => Text(
178                         secondModel.name,
179                         style: TextStyle(fontSize: 40.0),
180                         ),
181                     ),
182                     ),
183                     SizedBox(
184                     height: 10.0,
185                     ),
186                     Container(
187                     padding: const EdgeInsets.all(10.0),
188                     color: Colors.red[200],
189                     child: Consumer<SecondModelProvider>(
190                         builder: (context, secondModel, child) =>
RaisedButton(
191                         child: Text(
192                             'Get First Name',
193                             style: TextStyle(fontSize: 20.0),
194                         ),
195                         onPressed: () {
196                             secondModel.getFirstName();
197                         },
198                         ),
199                     ),
200                     ),
201             ],
202                 ),
203         ],
204             ),
205     ),
206
207     /// This trailing comma makes auto-formatting nicer for build
methods.
208     );
209 }
210 }
```

This part of the code has handled the Consumer section. Therefore, let us check that part first.

```
1 Container(
2                     padding: const EdgeInsets.all(10.0),
```

```
 3                     color: Colors.white30,
 4                     child: Consumer<SecondModelProvider>(
 5                         builder: (context, secondModel, child) => Text(
 6                         secondModel.name,
 7                         style: TextStyle(fontSize: 40.0),
 8                         ),
 9                     ),
10                     ),
11                 SizedBox(
12                 height: 10.0,
13                 ),
14                 Container(
15                 padding: const EdgeInsets.all(10.0),
16                 color: Colors.red[200],
17                     child: Consumer<SecondModelProvider>(
18                         builder: (context, secondModel, child) =>
RaisedButton(
19                         child: Text(
20                             'Get First Name',
21                             style: TextStyle(fontSize: 20.0),
22                         ),
23                         onPressed: () {
24                             secondModel.getFirstName();
25                         },
26                         ),
27                     ),
28                     ),
```

We are able to add another feature of state management through Provider. The second model Provider is a simple class.

```
 1 // second_model_provider.dart
 2
 3 import 'package:flutter/widgets.dart';
 4
 5 class SecondModelProvider with ChangeNotifier {
 6 String name = 'Some Name';
 7 int age = 0;
 8
 9 void getFirstName() {
10     name = 'Json';
11     print(name);
12     notifyListeners();
13 }
14 }
```

Next, if you proceed, you will find how Provider and Consumer work together. First, we have pressed the decrease button for 3 times. Next, we have pressed the 'Press me' button, and the 'Data Changed'. After that, finally, we have pressed the 'Get First Name' button, and the name appears on the screen.

Each Consumer widget has persisted its state, one button-press does not affect the other. The changed-data stays on the screen.

Before concluding this chapter, we will learn how we can separate business logic, application logic and screen-view.

To do that, we will keep our models inside the 'model' folder and keep our business logic there. We will keep our application logic inside the 'controller' folder, and finally we get the screen-view inside the 'view' folder.

For more Flutter related Articles and Resources

12. How to Organize Flutter Code, Model-View-Controller Patterns

I strongly prefer to organize Flutter code in a Model-View-Controller pattern.

This type of organization is necesary to make your code more readable and reusable. Although I've not written comments to make my every intention clear in the examples, I recommend readers to do that.

Take time, write your code along with detailed documentation, so that later you can come back and understand your code, your every step.

In the first part of my previous chapter, I have used model-view-controller pattern to manage an ephemeral, single widget stateful app, that allows users to take part in a quiz app.

Although it was not a full-blown, complete app, yet it could give you an idea how we could organize our code.

In this chapter, we'll learn that pattern in a detailed way. And this chapter is a continuation of the last chapter.

For more Flutter related Articles and Resources

The Role of Model

First of all, we need to update pubspec.yaml, because we want some special fonts to be displayed.

```
1 dependencies:
2 flutter:
3     sdk: flutter
4 provider: ^4.3.2
5
6 # To add assets to your application, add an assets section, like
this:
7 assets: [images/]
8
```

```
 9 fonts:
10 #    - family: Schyler
11 #      fonts:
12 #        - asset: fonts/Schyler.ttf
13 #        - asset: fonts/Schyler-Italic.ttf
14 #          style: italic
15     - family: Trajan Pro
16       fonts:
17         - asset: fonts/Trajan Pro Regular.ttf
18 #        - asset: fonts/TrajanPro_Bold.ttf
19 #          weight: 700
20     - family: Sacramento
21       fonts:
22 - asset: fonts/Sacramento-Regular.ttf
```

Next, we need two different models, ChangeNotifier, in our models folder. The first one is the following 'FirstModel' class.

```
 1 model/first_model.dart
 2
 3 import 'package:flutter/widgets.dart';
 4
 5 class FirstModel with ChangeNotifier {
 6 String name = 'name';
 7 void changeName() {
 8     name = 'Name Changed!';
 9     print(name);
10     notifyListeners();
11 }
12
13 void clearName() {
14     name = ' ';
15     print(name);
16     notifyListeners();
17 }
18 }
```

And the second model class is the 'MobileModel' that has a list of selected colors of which we will choose one for the background, and another for the mobile. We will display the mobile color on the foreground, and the background will be different.

Pressing the icon of the respective mobile will change the color of both – foreground and background. At the same time a text will be displayed to make us aware that foreground and background colors have been changed.

```
 1 model/mobile_model.dart
 2
 3 import 'package:flutter/material.dart';
 4 import 'package:flutter/widgets.dart';
 5
```

```
 6 class MobileModel with ChangeNotifier {
 7 String backgroundColorOfFirst = 'Background';
 8 String mobileColorOfFirst = 'Mobile';
 9 String backgroundColorOfSecond = 'Background';
10 String mobileColorOfSecond = 'Mobile';
11 List<Color> selection = [
12     Colors.yellow,
13     Colors.blue,
14     Colors.orange,
15     Colors.pinkAccent,
16     Colors.green,
17     Colors.limeAccent,
18 ];
19
20 void changeColorToPurple() {
21     backgroundColorOfFirst = 'Background \n Purle';
22     mobileColorOfFirst = 'Mobile \n White.';
23     selection[0] = Colors.purple;
24     selection[4] = Colors.white;
25     notifyListeners();
26 }
27
28 void changeColorToRed() {
29     backgroundColorOfSecond = 'Background \n Black';
30     mobileColorOfSecond = 'Mobile \n Red.';
31     selection[1] = Colors.black;
32     selection[5] = Colors.red;
33     notifyListeners();
34 }
35
36 void restoreOldColorOfFirstMobile() {
37     backgroundColorOfFirst = 'Background \n Yellow';
38     mobileColorOfFirst = 'Mobile \n Green.';
39     selection[0] = Colors.yellow;
40     selection[4] = Colors.green;
41     notifyListeners();
42 }
43
44 void restoreOldColorOfSecondMobile() {
45     backgroundColorOfSecond = 'Background \n Blue';
46     mobileColorOfSecond = 'Mobile \n Limeaccent.';
47     selection[1] = Colors.blue;
48     selection[5] = Colors.limeAccent;
49     notifyListeners();
50 }
51 }
```

The model classes are the sources of date. That data should be displayed on the
screen-view. Not only that, that data must be changed on the tap of the icon.

Therefore, we need some subscribers or Consumers who will get that data and pass them to the view accordingly.

Who will control that? The controllers. The controller will stay between model and view; the controllers' job is simple, it will play the role of the communicator who will manage the communication between model and view.

The data-source or model does not know where its data are going. The view does not know where from the data are coming. The controller knows everything. It controls every operation.

We have many controller widgets that will control different types of operations, such as one will control the foreground color, another will change background color, one controller will manage the text display, another will restore the value again, etc.

Even we have some controllers that will also decide what type of text style we will follow.

We have kept those controllers in two separate files inside 'controller' folder. One controller file is mobile specific. Another is page specific. The mobile specific controllers are as follows:

```dart
1 // controller/mobile_controller.dart
2
3 import 'package:first_flutter_app/model/mobile_model.dart';
4 import 'package:flutter/material.dart';
5 import 'package:flutter/widgets.dart';
6 import 'package:provider/provider.dart';
7
8 Widget changeColorButtonToPurple() => Column(
9     children: [
10        Container(
11        padding: const EdgeInsets.all(10.0),
12        child: Consumer<MobileModel>(
13            builder: (context, value, child) => Container(
14            padding: const EdgeInsets.all(15.0),
15            child: FloatingActionButton(
16                backgroundColor: value.selection[0],
17                onPressed: () {
18                value.changeColorToPurple();
19                },
20                child: Icon(
21                Icons.mobile_screen_share,
22                color: value.selection[4],
23                ),
24            ),
25            ),
26        ),
```

```dart
27          ),
28          Divider(
29          thickness: 2.0,
30          ),
31          Consumer<MobileModel>(
32          builder: (context, value, _) => Text(
33              value.backgroundColorOfFirst,
34              style: TextStyle(
35              fontFamily: 'Trajan Pro',
36              fontSize: 20.0,
37              fontWeight: FontWeight.bold,
38              ),
39          ),
40          ),
41          Divider(
42          thickness: 2.0,
43          ),
44          Consumer<MobileModel>(
45          builder: (context, value, _) =>
Text(value.mobileColorOfFirst,
46              style: TextStyle(
47                  fontFamily: 'Trajan Pro',
48                  fontSize: 20.0,
49                  fontWeight: FontWeight.bold,
50              )),
51          ),
52      ],
53      );
54
55 Widget changeColorButtonToRed() => Column(
56      children: [
57          Container(
58          padding: const EdgeInsets.all(10.0),
59          child: Consumer<MobileModel>(
60              builder: (context, value, child) => Container(
61              padding: const EdgeInsets.all(15.0),
62              child: FloatingActionButton(
63                  backgroundColor: value.selection[1],
64                  onPressed: () {
65                  value.changeColorToRed();
66                  },
67                  child: Icon(
68                  Icons.mobile_screen_share,
69                  color: value.selection[5],
70                  ),
71          ),
72          ),
73          ),
74          ),
75          Divider(
```

```dart
76                thickness: 2.0,
77                ),
78            Consumer<MobileModel>(
79            builder: (context, value, _) => Text(
80                value.backgroundColorOfSecond,
81                style: TextStyle(
82                fontFamily: 'Trajan Pro',
83                fontSize: 20.0,
84                fontWeight: FontWeight.bold,
85                ),
86            ),
87            ),
88          Divider(
89          thickness: 2.0,
90          ),
91            Consumer<MobileModel>(
92            builder: (context, value, _) =>
Text(value.mobileColorOfSecond,
93                style: TextStyle(
94                    fontFamily: 'Trajan Pro',
95                    fontSize: 20.0,
96                    fontWeight: FontWeight.bold,
97                )),
98            ),
99        ],
100        );
101
102 Widget restoreOldColorOfFirstMobile() => Container(
103      padding: const EdgeInsets.all(10.0),
104      child: Consumer<MobileModel>(
105          builder: (context, value, child) => Container(
106          padding: const EdgeInsets.all(10.0),
107          child: RaisedButton(
108            onPressed: () => value.restoreOldColorOfFirstMobile(),
109            child: Text(
110            'Restore',
111            style: TextStyle(
112                fontFamily: 'Sacramento',
113                fontSize: 25.0,
114                fontWeight: FontWeight.bold,
115            ),
116            ),
117        ),
118        ),
119      ),
120      );
121
122 Widget restoreOldColorOfSecondMobile() => Container(
123      padding: const EdgeInsets.all(10.0),
124      child: Consumer<MobileModel>(
```

```
125          builder: (context, value, child) => Container(
126            padding: const EdgeInsets.all(10.0),
127            child: RaisedButton(
128              onPressed: () => value.restoreOldColorOfSecondMobile(),
129              child: Text(
130              'Restore',
131              style: TextStyle(
132                fontFamily: 'Sacramento',
133                fontSize: 25.0,
134                fontWeight: FontWeight.bold,
135              ),
136              ),
137            ),
138          ),
139        ),
140      );
```

If we go through the above code, we will see several Consumers that have subscribed to those model classes. The role of these controllers are simple.

They will pass those data to the screen-view pages, which we will see in a minute.

Next goes the page-specific controller file:

```
1  // controller/second_home_page_controller.dart
2
3  import 'package:first_flutter_app/model/first_model.dart';
4  import 'package:flutter/material.dart';
5  import 'package:provider/provider.dart';
6
7  Widget textStyleTrajanPro(String trajan) => Text(
8      trajan,
9      style: TextStyle(
10         fontFamily: 'Trajan Pro',
11         fontSize: 35.0,
12         fontWeight: FontWeight.bold,
13     ),
14     textAlign: TextAlign.center,
15     );
16
17 Widget textStyleSacramento(String sacramento) => Text(
18     sacramento,
19     style: TextStyle(
20         fontFamily: 'Sacramento',
21         fontSize: 55.0,
22     ),
23     textAlign: TextAlign.center,
24     );
25
26 Widget changeNameButton() => Container(
27     padding: const EdgeInsets.all(30.0),
```

```
28      child: Consumer<FirstModel>(
29          builder: (context, value, child) => Container(
30          padding: const EdgeInsets.all(25.0),
31          child: RaisedButton(
32              child: Text(
33              'Change Name',
34              style: TextStyle(
35                  fontSize: 35.0,
36                  fontWeight: FontWeight.bold,
37              ),
38              ),
39              onPressed: () {
40              value.changeName();
41              },
42          ),
43          ),
44      ),
45      );
46
47 Widget clearNameButton() => Container(
48      padding: const EdgeInsets.all(30.0),
49      child: Consumer<FirstModel>(
50          builder: (context, value, child) => Container(
51          padding: const EdgeInsets.all(25.0),
52          child: RaisedButton(
53              child: Text(
54              'Clear Name',
55              style: TextStyle(
56                  fontSize: 35.0,
57                  fontWeight: FontWeight.bold,
58              ),
59              ),
60              onPressed: () {
61              value.clearName();
62              },
63          ),
64          ),
65      ),
66      );
```

In the above code, there are one or two Consumers, not as much as the mobile-specific controllers.

The Role of View

Before going to read the screen-view code, we will take a look at how our flutter application looks like:

Figure 12.1 – The first look of the application that we are going to build

Now we can scroll down to the bottom and see what are waiting for us. At the bottom part, we have two buttons, and below those buttons, we have two mobile icons and respective text that tells us about the foreground and background colors.

If we click the 'Change Name' button, it will display a text 'Name Changed'. Just below that text we have the 'Clear name' button. Pressing that button will clear the text (Figure 8.9).

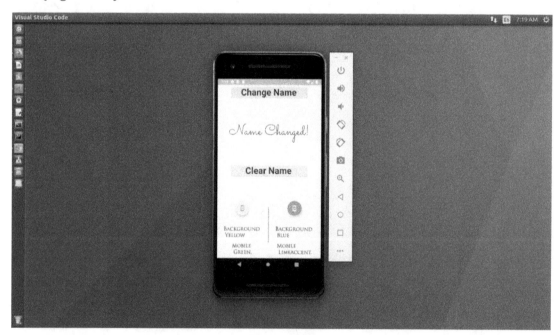

Figure 12.2 – The bottom part of our application

At the very bottom two mobile icons are visible. We can also see the name of the foreground and background color in text. Tapping any icon will change the foreground and background color, and at the same time, the description of color displayed in text will also change.

Finally, let us see the screen-view page and the main method.

```
 1 // view/second_home_app.dart
 2
 3
 4 import
'package:first_flutter_app/controller/mobile_controller.dart';
 5 import
'package:first_flutter_app/controller/second_home_page_controller.dart'
;
 6 import 'package:first_flutter_app/model/first_model.dart';
 7 import 'package:flutter/material.dart';
 8 import 'package:provider/provider.dart';
 9
10 class SecondHomeAppPage extends StatelessWidget {
11 @override
12 Widget build(BuildContext context) {
13     return MaterialApp(
14     debugShowCheckedModeBanner: false,
15     title: 'Second Provider Example',
16     home: Scaffold(
17         body: SafeArea(
18         child: ListView(
19             children: [
20             textStyleSacramento('Provider Examples'),
21             Container(
22                 padding: const EdgeInsets.all(20.0),
23                 child: Image.asset(
24                 'images/sea1.jpg',
25                 width: 300,
26                 ),
27             ),
28             textStyleTrajanPro('We can add humongous widget tree
below...'),
29             changeNameButton(),
30             Container(
31                 padding: const EdgeInsets.all(30.0),
32                 child: textStyleSacramento(
33                     Provider.of<FirstModel>(context, listen:
true).name),
34             ),
35             clearNameButton(),
36             SizedBox(
37                 height: 10.0,
38             ),
```

```dart
39              Row(
40                  mainAxisAlignment: MainAxisAlignment.spaceEvenly,
41                  children: [
42                  changeColorButtonToPurple(),
43                  VerticalLine(),
44                  changeColorButtonToRed(),
45                  ],
46              ),
47              SizedBox(
48                  height: 10.0,
49              ),
50              Row(
51                  mainAxisAlignment: MainAxisAlignment.spaceEvenly,
52                  children: [
53                  restoreOldColorOfFirstMobile(),
54                  VerticalLine(),
55                  restoreOldColorOfSecondMobile(),
56                  ],
57              ),
58              ],
59          ),
60          ),
61      ),
62      );
63 }
64 }
65
66 class VerticalLine extends StatelessWidget {
67 const VerticalLine({
68      Key key,
69 }) : super(key: key);
70
71 @override
72 Widget build(BuildContext context) {
73      return Center(
74      child: Container(
75          height: MediaQuery.of(context).size.height * 0.2,
76          width: 3,
77          color: Colors.black45,
78      ),
79      );
80 }
81 }
82
83 class HorizontalLine extends StatelessWidget {
84 const HorizontalLine({
85      Key key,
86 }) : super(key: key);
87
88 @override
```

```
89 Widget build(BuildContext context) {
90     return Center(
91     child: Container(
92         width: MediaQuery.of(context).size.width * 0.2,
93         height: 3,
94         color: Colors.black45,
95     ),
96     );
97 }
98 }
```

And the main method is as the following where we have used multi Provider :

```
 1 // main.dart
 2
 3 import 'package:first_flutter_app/model/first_model.dart';
 4 import 'package:first_flutter_app/view/second_home_app.dart';
 5 import 'package:flutter/material.dart';
 6 import 'package:provider/provider.dart';
 7
 8 import 'model/mobile_model.dart';
 9
10 void main() {
11 runApp(
12     MultiProvider(
13     providers: [
14         ChangeNotifierProvider(create: (context) => FirstModel()),
15         ChangeNotifierProvider(create: (context) => MobileModel()),
16     ],
17     child: SecondHomeAppPage(),
18     ),
19 );
20 }
```

Now, we can press the 'Change Name' button, and get the text. Let us do that, and take a look at the lower bottom part.

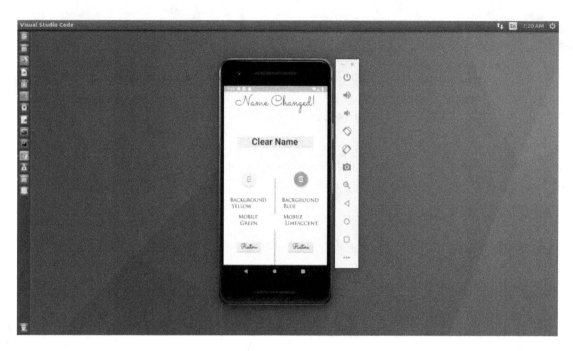

Figure 12.3 – The lower bottom part of our application

Next, we will start operating at the lower bottom part. Remember, we have already pressed the 'Change Name' button,and got the text displayed on the top of the screen-view.

Now we are going to change the first mobile icon color, foreground and background, both.

Let us see the image first, after that, we will discuss the code.

Figure 12.4 – The first mobile icon's foreground and background color have been changed and it has been reflected on the below text

We can clearly watch that the first mobile icon's foreground has been changed to white from green; at the same time the background color has been changed from yellow to purple.

Let us see this coding part in the mobile model class.

```
1 void changeColorToPurple() {
2     backgroundColorOfFirst = 'Background \n Purle';
3     mobileColorOfFirst = 'Mobile \n White.';
4     selection[0] = Colors.purple;
5     selection[4] = Colors.white;
6     notifyListeners();
7 }
```

After that, we will take a look at the related mobile controller's coding part.

```
1 Widget changeColorButtonToPurple() => Column(
2     children: [
3         Container(
4         padding: const EdgeInsets.all(10.0),
5         child: Consumer<MobileModel>(
6             builder: (context, value, child) => Container(
7             padding: const EdgeInsets.all(15.0),
8             child: FloatingActionButton(
9                 backgroundColor: value.selection[0],
10                onPressed: () {
11                value.changeColorToPurple();
12                },
```

```
13                   child: Icon(
14                   Icons.mobile_screen_share,
15                   color: value.selection[4],
16                   ),
17             ),
18             ),
19         ),
20         ),
21         Divider(
22         thickness: 2.0,
23         ),
24         Consumer<MobileModel>(
25         builder: (context, value, _) => Text(
26             value.backgroundColorOfFirst,
27             style: TextStyle(
28             fontFamily: 'Trajan Pro',
29             fontSize: 20.0,
30             fontWeight: FontWeight.bold,
31             ),
32         ),
33         ),
34         Divider(
35         thickness: 2.0,
36         ),
37         Consumer<MobileModel>(
38         builder: (context, value, _) =>
Text(value.mobileColorOfFirst,
39             style: TextStyle(
40                 fontFamily: 'Trajan Pro',
41                 fontSize: 20.0,
42                 fontWeight: FontWeight.bold,
43             )),
44         ),
45     ],
46     );
```

And, finally we can watch the screen-view page part, where we have called this controller.

```
1 Row(
2                   mainAxisAlignment: MainAxisAlignment.spaceEvenly,
3                   children: [
4                   changeColorButtonToPurple(),
5                   VerticalLine(),
6                   changeColorButtonToRed(),
7                   ],
8               ),
```

In the same row, we can call both controllers that will change the foreground and background color.

Therefore, in the next image, we will see that the second mobile icon's foreground and background color have also been changed, because we have tapped the second icon.

Figure 12.5 – The second mobile icon's foreground and background color have been changed

We can clearly see that the second mobile icon's foreground changed to red, and the background changed to black. The below text has also displayed the name of the color respectively.

One thing is also evident, although two controllers belong to the same Row widget, one change does not affect the other.

Our next step will be to restore the old data. First, we will click the restore button below the first mobile icon. Secondly, we will click the second restore button below the second mobile icon.

And finally, we will click the 'Clear name' button on the upper half of the screen. It will first restore the old color of the first mobile icon, next, it will change the second mobile icon; and finally it will clear the 'name' that was stuck on the upper half of the screen.

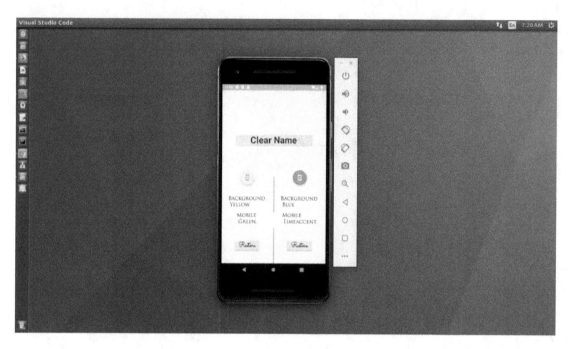

Figure 12.6 – The final screen shot of our application

We have learned how we can use Provider package, and Consumer widget to manage state efficiently. We have also learned how without rebuilding the whole widget tree, we can change and persist state of our application.

In the next chapter, we will learn how to navigate from one screen to others and come back with the help of Provider and keeping our State intact!

Want to read more Flutter related Articles and resources?

For more Flutter related Articles and Resources

13. ChangeNotifier and Provider context read and watch, when to use and how to use

If we want to avoid widget rebuilding in Flutter, the rule of thumb is avoid stateful widget. And the golden solution is also available.

Use ChangeNotifier native class of Flutter along with Provider package.

Although for a small app using stateful widget is okay. But for a full blown, complicated app architecture always avoid stateful widget, and always try to stick with the Provider package.

Why?

That will help you to avoid widget rebuilding. When you use ChangeNotifier native Flutter class with Provider, value changes but widget is not rebuilt.

Hence the loading time increases. In any app development, managing time complexity makes all the difference.

In this chapter, we're going to learn how we can avoid widget-rebuilding in Flutter, reducing the loading time.

In the previous chapter we've seen how one can build a small quiz app in Flutter. Since it was a small app, we had used stateful widget.

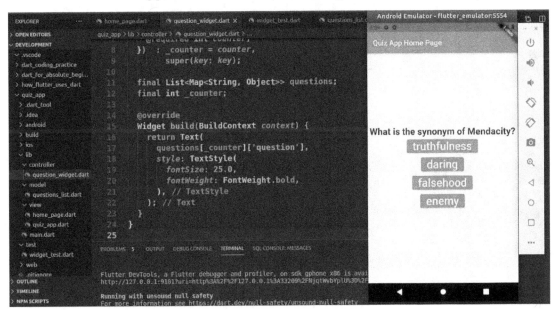

Figure 13.1 – A Quiz App using stateful widget

As a result, each time we click the button, the whole widget tree is rebuilt. Remember, it's a small app, so we don't have an expensive parent widget tree on the top of the widget where we return the changed value.

In reality or to be precise in the professional app building world, it never happens.

What I feel, using stateful widget is unnecessary. Moreover, for a small app it's okay. But what will happen when we will have an expensive parent widget tree?

While rebuilding a single widget, it will actually rebuild the whole parent widget tree.

We should avoid this imbroglio to enhance our fluttering performance.

For more Flutter related Articles and Resources

How can I improve my fluttering performance?

Use Provider package. Provider is a wrapper class of Inherited widget. However, with the help of Change notifier it helps us to overcome the limitations of stateful widget.

We don't have to rebuild the widget anymore.

Let us try to make the whole concept a little bit simpler than it seems. Take a look at the image below.

We have rebuilt the previous quiz app using Provider package this time.

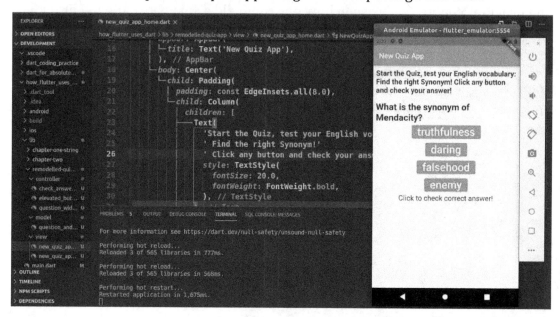

Figure 13.2 – The same Quiz App using stateless widget and provider changenotifier

As you can see, there are several options from which you can choose the correct synonym of the word Mendacity.

Clicking any button will take you to the next question and, besides it will also display the correct answer.

Therefore we need to tackle three changes at a single time! Although these changes take place in different widgets, but not a single widget is rebuilt.

The next image will show you how our app is working fine.

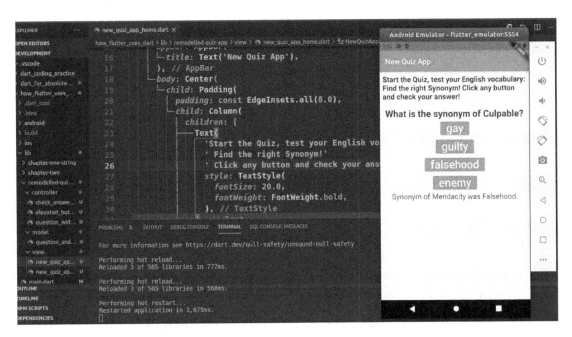

Figure 13.3 – The Quiz App using provider change notifier

It certainly improves our fluttering performance because we've used ChangeNotifier with Provider.

In the above image, it's clearly visible that the next screenshot shows us the next question and at the same time,it also displays the synonym of the previous word - Mendacity.

How to avoid the anti-pattern and stick to the correct design pattern in Flutter?

This time we've used provider package and follow the correct design pattern principle. So with the click of the button we see three values simultaneously change.

At the top appears the new question. In the Elevated button text four new synonyms appear, and finally, the app displays the correct answer of the previous question.

With reference to our previous query, whether we can avoid the unnecessary widget rebuilding, the answer is, yes, we have achieved that in this quiz app.

Before diving deep into the code let me tell you one thing. You'll get the whole code snippet in my GitHub repository.

The first code repository with stateful widget

The second code repository with statless widget and provider package

How have we got rid of widget rebuild in Flutter?

The code snippet is fairly long. So let us break it down and try to understand how things take place.

We keep the providers above the app. Although it has a different reason involving the test purpose, but still it has another advantage.

As we have already said, Provider is the wrapper class of inherited widget.

Here is the main method, the entry point of our app.

```
1 import 'package:flutter/material.dart';
2 import 'package:provider/provider.dart';
3 import './remodelled-quiz-app/model/question_and_answer_model.dart';
4 import './remodelled-quiz-app/view/new_quiz_app.dart';
5
6 void main() {
7 runApp(
8 /// Providers are above [NewQuizApp] instead of inside it
9 MultiProvider(
10 providers: [
11 // ChangeNotifierProvider(create: (_) => Counter()),
12 // ChangeNotifierProvider(create: (_) => MyCounter()),
13 ChangeNotifierProvider(create: (_) => QuestionAndAnswerModel()),
14 ],
15 child: NewQuizApp(),
16 ),
17 );
18 }
```

As we have already created three directories – controller, model and view, we keep our NewQuizApp widget in the view directory.

```
1 import 'package:flutter/material.dart';
2 import './new_quiz_app_home.dart';
3
4 class NewQuizApp extends StatelessWidget {
5 const NewQuizApp({Key key}) : super(key: key);
6
7 @override
8 Widget build(BuildContext context) {
9 return MaterialApp(
10 home: NewQuizAppHome(),
11 );
12 }
13 }
```

The NewQuizAppHome widget is the main user interface that we've already seen in the above images.

How do you change the state in Flutter?

Whenever we want to change the state in Flutter we follow some rules.

What are the rules regarding state change?

Usually we notify the framework that the internal state of an object has changed. To do that we need to change the internal state of a State object, making the change in a function that we pass to setState(){}.

Here we will take a different route.

In our model directory we have a class QuestionAndAnswerModel, which extends ChangeNotifier class.

What is ChangeNotifier?

According to the Flutter documentation:

```
1 ChangeNotifier is a simple class included in the Flutter SDK which
provides change n\
2 otification to its listeners. In other words, if something is a
ChangeNotifier, you \
3 can subscribe to its changes.
```

One thing is clear. Our quiz app values, that means questions, answers, etc can subscribe its changes.

```
 1 import 'package:flutter/widgets.dart';
 2
 3 class QuestionAndAnswerModel extends ChangeNotifier {
 4 List<Map<String, Object>> questions = [
 5 {
 6 'question': 'What is the synonym of Mendacity?',
 7 'answers': ['truthfulness', 'daring', 'falsehood', 'enemy'],
 8 },
 9 {
10 'question': 'What is the synonym of Culpable?',
11 'answers': ['gay', 'guilty', 'falsehood', 'enemy'],
12 },
13 {
14 'question': 'What is the synonym of Rapacious?',
15 'answers': ['guilty', 'daring', 'falsehood', 'greedy'],
16 },
17 ];
18 int counter = 0;
19
20 String answerChecking = 'Click to check correct answer!';
21
22 void incrementCounter() {
23 counter++;
24 notifyListeners();
25
26 if (counter > 2) {
27 counter = 0;
28 }
29 checkAnswer();
```

```
30 }
31
32 void checkAnswer() {
33 if (counter == 0) {
34 answerChecking = 'Synonym of Rapacious was Greedy.';
35 } else if (counter == 1) {
36 answerChecking = 'Synonym of Mendacity was Falsehood.';
37 } else if (counter == 2) {
38 answerChecking = 'Synonym of Culpable was Guilty.';
39 } else {
40 answerChecking = 'Click to check correct answer!';
41 }
42 }
43 }
```

Now we're going to use the Provider package.

What is the difference between stateful and stateless widget in Flutter?

If you have already read the previous article where we have used the stateful widget to accomplish the same task, you will distinguish between these two widgets.

Now we're going to have the main interface NewQuizAppHome where we use Provider read and watch method for the first time.

```
 1 import 'package:flutter/material.dart';
 2 import 'package:provider/provider.dart';
 3 import '../controller/question_widget.dart';
 4 import '../controller/check_answer_widget.dart';
 5 import '../controller/elevated_button_widget.dart';
 6 import '../model/question_and_answer_model.dart';
 7
 8 class NewQuizAppHome extends StatelessWidget {
 9 const NewQuizAppHome({Key key}) : super(key: key);
10
11 @override
12 Widget build(BuildContext context) {
13 return Container(
14 child: Scaffold(
15 appBar: AppBar(
16 title: Text('New Quiz App'),
17 ),
18 body: Center(
19 child: Padding(
20 padding: const EdgeInsets.all(8.0),
21 child: Column(
22 children: [
23 Text(
24 'Start the Quiz, test your English vocabulary:'
25 ' Find the right Synonym!'
26 ' Click any button and check your answer!',
```

```
27 style: TextStyle(
28 fontSize: 20.0,
29 fontWeight: FontWeight.bold,
30 ),
31 ),
32 SizedBox(height: 20.0),
33 QuestionWidget(
34 /// static method Provider.of<T>(context), which will behave
similarly to watch
35 ///
36 questions:
37 Provider.of<QuestionAndAnswerModel>(context).questions,
38 // questions: context.watch<QuestionAndAnswerModel>().questions,
39 counter: context.watch<QuestionAndAnswerModel>().counter,
40 ),
41 ...(context.watch<QuestionAndAnswerModel>().questions[context
42 .watch<QuestionAndAnswerModel>()
43 .counter]['answers'] as List<String>)
44 .map(
45 (answer) => ElevatedButtonWidget(
46 answer: answer,
47 ),
48 )
49 .toList(),
50 CheckAnswerWidget(),
51 ],
52 ),
53 ),
54 ),
55 ),
56 );
57 }
58 }
```

According to the Provider package documentation:

```
1 It's worth noting that context.read<T>() won't make widget rebuild
when the value ch\
2 anges and cannot be called inside StatelessWidget.build/State.build.
On the other ha\
3 nd, it can be freely called outside of these methods.
```

You can use both:

```
1 Or to use the static method Provider.of<T>(context), which will
behave similarly to \
2 watch and when you pass false to the listen parameter like
Provider.of<T>(context,li\
3 sten: false) it will behave similar to read.
```

As Flutter encourages to break the app design into smaller segments, we keep three controllers in separate directory.

What does provider do in Flutter?

I hope you have already got the answer. Yet it is always better we show the code.

First the QuestionWidget, where we're going to have the list of questions and the index through which we can change the question by the press of button.

```
 1 import 'package:flutter/material.dart';
 2 import 'package:provider/provider.dart';
 3 import '../model/question_and_answer_model.dart';
 4
 5 class QuestionWidget extends StatelessWidget {
 6 const QuestionWidget({
 7 Key key,
 8 @required this.questions,
 9 @required this.counter,
10 }) : super(key: key);
11
12 final List<Map<String, Object>> questions;
13 final int counter;
14
15 @override
16 Widget build(BuildContext context) {
17 return Text(
18 context
19 .watch<QuestionAndAnswerModel>()
20 .questions[context.watch<QuestionAndAnswerModel>().counter]
21 ['question'],
22 style: TextStyle(
23 fontSize: 25.0,
24 fontWeight: FontWeight.bold,
25 ),
26 );
27 }
28 }
```

The following line is important.

```
1
context.watch<QuestionAndAnswerModel>().questions[context.watch<Questio
nAndAnswerMod\
2 el>().counter]['question'],
```

Here the type is QuestionAndAnswerModel.

The same way, we can watch and check the correct answer.

```
 1 import 'package:flutter/material.dart';
 2 import 'package:provider/provider.dart';
 3 import '../model/question_and_answer_model.dart';
 4
 5 class CheckAnswerWidget extends StatelessWidget {
 6 const CheckAnswerWidget({
 7 Key key,
 8 }) : super(key: key);
 9
10 @override
11 Widget build(BuildContext context) {
12 return Text(
13 context.watch<QuestionAndAnswerModel>().answerChecking,
14 style: TextStyle(
15 fontSize: 20.0,
16 ),
17 );
18 }
19 }
```

For the Elevated button we're going to use context.read<T>.

Provider helps you to avoid rebuilding widgets

Whenever we press the Elevated button it calls the incrementCounter() method, which in turn calls another method that we have seen in our model class.

However, this doesn't involve any kind of widget rebuilding. That is the advantage of Provider package.

```
 1 import 'package:flutter/material.dart';
 2 import 'package:provider/provider.dart';
 3 import '../model/question_and_answer_model.dart';
 4
 5 class ElevatedButtonWidget extends StatelessWidget {
 6 ElevatedButtonWidget({Key key, this.answer}) : super(key: key);
 7 final String answer;
 8
 9 @override
10 Widget build(BuildContext context) {
11 return ElevatedButton(
12 /// when you pass false to the listen parameter
13 /// like Provider.of<T>(context,listen: false) it will behave
similar to read
14 ///
15 onPressed: () =>
16 // context.read<QuestionAndAnswerModel>().incrementCounter(),
17 Provider.of<QuestionAndAnswerModel>(context, listen: false)
18 .incrementCounter(),
19 child: Text(
20 answer,
```

```
21 style: TextStyle(
22 fontSize: 30.0,
23 ),
24 ),
25 );
26 }
27 }
```

14. Provider best practices: How to reduce widget rebuilds

How do we use a provider in Flutter? Well, we have seen many examples already. In fact, there is nothing new in it.

However, the question is what is the most efficient way to use Provider package?

Another question is how we can use Flutter ChangeNotifier class along with Provider, so that it gives us the best result.

Will that really reduce widget re-building and enhance the efficiency of our Flutter App?

The answer is – yes! It does.

In this chapter we will look into that matter. Not only that, we will also show proof of it. To prove that Provider is more efficient than stateful widget, we have used Android Studio Flutter Inspector and Flutter Performance,which will track the widget rebuilding.

These tools will show you how many widgets are rebuilt when user presses a button. With reference to the provider's best usage patterns we will also learn how to organize our code.

How do you use a provider in Flutter?

In a large application, there could be many types of provider. The generics, the value inside <> brackets point to a particular provider.

In fact, according to the generics, Flutter knows what "type" of provider it is looking for.

Once it knows, Flutter goes up the widget tree until it finds the provided value.

Once Flutter gets the provider, either it uses watch method to reflect the changed property or read method to change the event or, in other words, call the method on it.

Therefore how to use flutter provider doesn't concern us. We want the proof that provider works better and faster than stateful widget.

So let's start with a simple stateful widget example where user presses a button that increments the value. In this example we will see how a stateful widget takes a toll on the whole widget tree.

When do I use stateful widget? Or, should I?

In my opinion, stateful widget doesn't make any sense. In fact, when a stateless widget does the same job, why you should use that?

Why not, I am going to show you in a minute.

If you search Internet, it says many things about stateful widget. People say stateful widget is useful when the part of the user interface you are describing can change dynamically.

We can do the same with the help of provider package, CgangeNotifier class and a stateless widget.

Just like too much sunlight takes a heavy toll on your skin, a stateful widget has a serious effect on the whole widget tree. Moreover, that bad effect starts rebuilding widgets from the very top. That is from your home page, then it rebuilds the scaffold widget, and all the child widgets under it.

Now under Scaffold widget, whatever widgets you have, all are rebuilt for a press of button!

Does it sound good?

I don't think so.

But give us a proof!

How does stateful widget rebuild the whole tree?

Let us first consider a simple stateful widget example.

```
1 import 'package:flutter/material.dart';
2
3 void main() {
4 runApp(MyApp());
5 }
6
7 class MyApp extends StatelessWidget {
8 // This widget is the root of your application.
9 @override
10 Widget build(BuildContext context) {
11 return MaterialApp(
12 title: 'Flutter Demo',
```

```dart
13 theme: ThemeData(
14 primarySwatch: Colors.blue,
15 ),
16 home: MyHomePage(title: 'Flutter Demo Home Page'),
17 );
18 }
19 }
20
21 class MyHomePage extends StatefulWidget {
22 MyHomePage({Key key, this.title}) : super(key: key);
23
24 final String title;
25
26 @override
27 _MyHomePageState createState() => _MyHomePageState();
28 }
29
30 class _MyHomePageState extends State<MyHomePage> {
31 int _counter = 0;
32
33 void _incrementCounter() {
34 setState(() {
35
36 _counter++;
37 });
38 }
39
40 @override
41 Widget build(BuildContext context) {
42
43 return Scaffold(
44 appBar: AppBar(
45
46 title: Text(widget.title),
47 ),
48 body: Center(
49
50 child: Column(
51
52 mainAxisAlignment: MainAxisAlignment.center,
53 children: <Widget>[
54 Text(
55 'You have pushed the button this many times:',
56 ),
57 Text(
58 '$_counter',
59 style: Theme.of(context).textTheme.headline4,
60 ),
61 ],
62 ),
```

```
63 ),
64 floatingActionButton: FloatingActionButton(
65 onPressed: _incrementCounter,
66 tooltip: 'Increment',
67 child: Icon(Icons.add),
68 ), // This trailing comma makes auto-formatting nicer for build
methods.
69 );
70 }
71 }
```

Now we have pressed the counter button six times. This press of button will rebuild the Floating action button widget, and even the Icon widget. We cannot even avoid if we use provider package.

But why it should start rebuilding from the top widget?

We must demonstrate to establish the truth of our conjecture.

What proof do we have? The next image shows it.

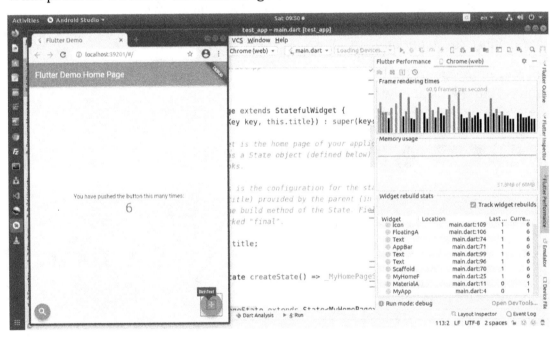

Figure 14.1 – The whole widget tree is rebuilt when we use a stateful widget

Let me tell you about this image first. It demonstrates a simple stateful flutter app on the left side. That indicates we have pressed the button six times.

On the right side of Android Studio, we have opened the Flutter Performance window and ticked the "Track Widget rebuilds", which shows us the proof.

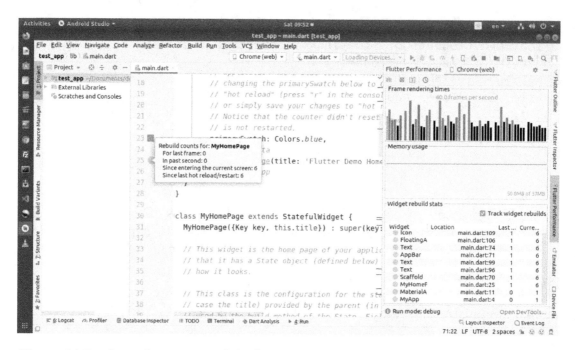

Figure 14.2 – As we have pressed the button 6 times in the Stateful widget, the topmost MyHOmePage widget has been also hot reloaded or restarted 6 times resulting in heavy memory consumption

From MyHomePage to Scaffold to AppBar, everything has been rebuilt six times. Can we have a close look at how widget rebuilds?

Sure we can have a closer look than before.

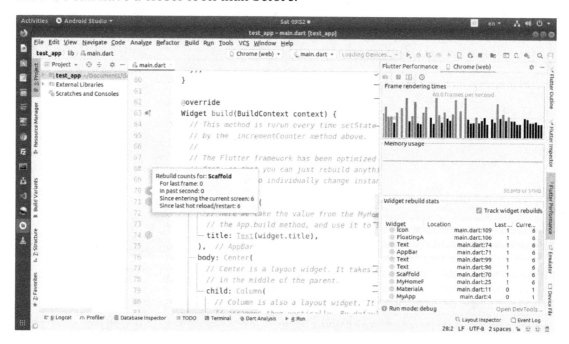

Figure 14.3 – As you see the Scaffold has also been rebuilt 6 times for a the press of a button

It clearly shows that MyHomePage has been rebuilt six time for a singular button pressing. And that happens to Scaffold widget also.

However, when we will use provider package, this will never happen. We'll see the proof in a minute.

We can have more proof that will show you that in the similar way Scaffold has been rebuilt six times too!

But we have enough proof. Now let's concentrate on provider package. How do we use provider efficiently so that we can avoid the whole widget tree rebuilding?

Now, we come to the main point.

First of all we will demonstrate how we can stop this bad effect on our flutter app. If we use a stateful widget, a single button-press rebuilds the whole widget tree and consumes a hell lot of memory.

We've just seen that effect.

Moreover, for a complex app structure using a stateful widget seriously affects the speed.

Therefore, we must find the best solution. Our first target is simple. We cannot stop the widget rebuilds totally. But we can try to make it sure that less widgets are rebuilt in the process.

Well, what does that mean actually?

It means we can place one type of provider inside a one type of widget and another type of widget inside another type of widget.

The golden rule is break your app in many small chunks. One model class should have one task.

That will enhance the efficiency of our flutter app.

Model, View, Controller and Provider

Inside our model folder we have three separate class that extends change notifier. Each method will notify the listeners.

Now, the bottom-most widget could be the subscriber of that notification. At that widget, one press of button changes one value. Moreover, while doing so it doesn't rebuild the whole widget tree structure.

This time, our main app page is not rebuilt. Remember the top-most MyHomePage widget in our previous stateful widget example.

We have a solid proof indeed. However, before demonstrate the proof we should look at the code organization first.

Firstly, we have a NumberModel class. It has one task to do. If you press the button, the counter value increases by 2.

```
 1 import 'package:flutter/material.dart';
 2
 3 class NumberModel extends ChangeNotifier {
 4 int _counter = 0;
 5 int get counter => _counter;
 6 void incrementNumberByTwo() {
 7 _counter = _counter + 2;
 8 notifyListeners();
 9 }
10 }
```

Next, we have NameChangeModel that changes a name from 'Sanjib' to 'John'.

```
 1 import 'package:flutter/material.dart';
 2
 3 class NameChangeModel extends ChangeNotifier {
 4 String _name = 'Sanjib';
 5 String get name => _name;
 6 void changeName() {
 7 _name = 'John';
 8 notifyListeners();
 9 }
10 }
```

Finally, we have NameClearModel class that helps us to get the previous name back to the screen.

```
 1 import 'package:flutter/material.dart';
 2
 3 class NameClearModel extends ChangeNotifier {
 4 String _name = ' ';
 5 String get name => _name;
 6 void clearName() {
 7 _name = 'Sanjib';
 8 notifyListeners();
 9 }
10 }
```

Who will subscribe to these notifications? The First row widget will listen to Number Model

According to our design patterns, the controller folder has three related Widgets that will subscribe to these notifications.

Let us see one by one.

The FirstRowWidget has code like the following:

```
 1 import 'package:flutter/material.dart';
 2 import 'package:provider/provider.dart';
 3 import '../model/number_model.dart';
 4
 5
 6 class FirstRowWidget extends StatelessWidget {
 7 const FirstRowWidget({
 8 Key key,
 9 }) : super(key: key);
10
11 @override
12 Widget build(BuildContext context) {
13 return Row(
14 mainAxisSize: MainAxisSize.min,
15 children: [
16 Expanded(
17 child: Padding(
18 padding: EdgeInsets.all(20.0),
19 child: Column(
20 children: [
21 Text('You have pushed this button this time!'),
22
23 /// this is our one [NumberModel] listener
24 /// watch() will reflect the change in number
25 /// as one presses the button
26 ///
27 Text('${context.watch<NumberModel>().counter}'),
28 /**
29 * ElevatedButton(
30 /// this is our another [NumberModel] listener
31 /// read() will fire the event the changes the number
32 /// by adding 2
33 ///
34 onPressed: () =>
35 context.read<NumberModel>().incrementNumberByTwo(),
36 child: Text('Increment'),
37 ),
38 */
39 FloatingActionButton(
40 onPressed: () => context.read<NumberModel>().incrementNumberByTwo(),
41 tooltip: 'Increment',
42 child: Icon(Icons.add),
43 ), // Th
44 ],
45 ),
46 ),
47 ),
48 ],
```

```
49 );
50 }
51 }
```

The associated image will show the changed look.

Figure 14.4 – The changed look of flutter app

Now we get the changed look of flutter app with the help of provider package.

On the left side we can see that we have pressed the button 4 times, so we've got 8. And on the right hand side of the screen, we can see how many widgets get rebuilt.

We'll see more advantage of using provider package in a minute.

Figure 14.5 – Now a single pressing of a button results into FirstRowWidget rebuild only! That also indicates less memory usage

The Second Row Widget will listen to the Name Change Model

Just like before, this time we will press the second button to change the name 'Sanjib' to 'John'.

To make it happen, the second row widget will listen to the name change model.

```
1 import 'package:flutter/material.dart';
2 import 'package:provider/provider.dart';
3 import '../model/name_change_model.dart';
4
5
6 class SecondRowWidget extends StatelessWidget {
7 const SecondRowWidget({
8 Key key,
9 }) : super(key: key);
10
11 @override
12 Widget build(BuildContext context) {
13 return Row(
14 mainAxisSize: MainAxisSize.min,
15 children: [
16 Expanded(
17 child: Padding(
18 padding: EdgeInsets.all(20.0),
19 child: Column(
20 children: [
21 Text('${context.watch<NameChangeModel>().name}'),
```

```
22 /**
23 * ElevatedButton(
24 /// this is our another [NumberModel] listener
25 /// read() will fire the event the changes the number
26 /// by adding 2
27 ///
28 onPressed: () =>
29 context.read<NumberModel>().incrementNumberByTwo(),
30 child: Text('Increment'),
31 ),
32 */
33 FloatingActionButton(
34 onPressed: () => context.read<NameChangeModel>().changeName(),
35 tooltip: 'Increment',
36 child: Icon(Icons.add),
37 ), // Th
38 ],
39 ),
40 ),
41 ),
42 ],
43 );
44 }
45 }
```

The next image will demonstrate how the process of widget rebuilds have been restricted in a great way.

Figure 14.6 – Provider helps reducing widget rebuilds, even pressing two buttons subsequently result into less memory usage

This time we have reduced the number of widget rebuilds and it's clearly visible. Not only that, if you compare the red bar of Frame rendering times, with the stateful widget, you will see the difference.

This time, when we click the button to increment number, only First row widget gets rebuilt. It is clearly visible in the image.

Next, we will see the code of third row widget.

Third Row Widget listens to Name Clear Model

Now, things are getting interesting. We have pressed the button to change the name, and the second row widget is the subscriber.

The third row widget subscribes to the name clear model event.

Here is the code:

```
1 import 'package:flutter/material.dart';
2 import 'package:provider/provider.dart';
3 import '../model/name_clear_model.dart';
4
5
6 class ThirdRowWidget extends StatelessWidget {
7 const ThirdRowWidget({Key key}) : super(key: key);
8
9 @override
10 Widget build(BuildContext context) {
11 return Row(
12 mainAxisSize: MainAxisSize.min,
13 children: [
14 Expanded(
15 child: Padding(
16 padding: EdgeInsets.all(20.0),
17 child: Column(
18 children: [
19 Text('${context.watch<NameClearModel>().name}'),
20 /**
21 * ElevatedButton(
22 /// this is our another [NumberModel] listener
23 /// read() will fire the event the changes the number
24 /// by adding 2
25 ///
26 onPressed: () =>
27 context.read<NumberModel>().incrementNumberByTwo(),
28 child: Text('Increment'),
29 ),
30 */
31 FloatingActionButton(
32 onPressed: () => context.read<NameClearModel>().clearName(),
33 tooltip: 'Increment',
```

```
34 child: Icon(Icons.add),
35 ), // Th
36 ],
37 ),
38 ),
39 ),
40 ],
41 );
42 }
43 }
```

If you press the third button, the third row widget will listen to the event declared in clear name model.

Let's see the last image where we will see that every button-press restricts the unnecessary widget rebuilds. Scaffold, AppBar widgets have never been rebuilt, although it happened in the case of stateful widget.

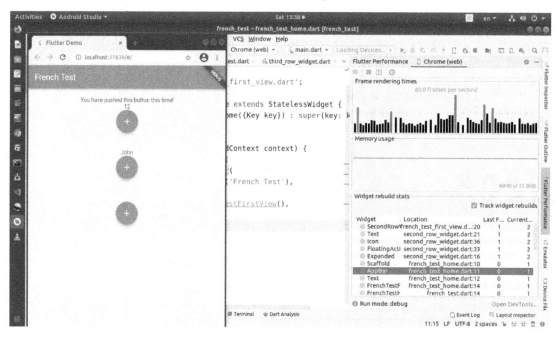

Figure 14.7 – Restricting widget rebuilds with the help of provider

On the right hand side, we can clearly see that Scaffold and AppBar widgets have never been rebuilt whenever we've pressed the button. How many times we have pressed, that really doesn't matter. The widget rebuilds are restricted in great amount.

Finally the view folder and main method

We've split the stateless widgets into more reusable widgets. As a result, the the view folder has three widgets that chain to one another.

We'll see them to understand the code organization.

Let us start with the main method.

```
1 import 'package:flutter/material.dart';
2 import 'package:provider/provider.dart';
3 import 'model/number_model.dart';
4 import 'model/name_change_model.dart';
5 import 'model/name_clear_model.dart';
6 import 'view/french_test.dart';
7
8 void main() {
9 runApp(
10 /// Providers are above [FrenchTestApp] instead of inside it
11 MultiProvider(
12 providers: [
13 ChangeNotifierProvider(create: (_) => NumberModel()),
14 ChangeNotifierProvider(create: (_) => NameChangeModel()),
15 ChangeNotifierProvider(create: (_) => NameClearModel()),
16 ],
17 child: FrenchTestApp(),
18 ),
19 );
20 }
```

We've kept our three providers above our flutter app.

Next, we'll see the code of FrenchTestApp in view folder.

```
1 import 'package:flutter/material.dart';
2 import 'french_test_home.dart';
3
4 class FrenchTestApp extends StatelessWidget {
5 // This widget is the root of your application.
6 @override
7 Widget build(BuildContext context) {
8 return MaterialApp(
9 title: 'Flutter Demo',
10 theme: ThemeData(
11 // This is the theme of your application.
12 primarySwatch: Colors.blue,
13 ),
14 home: FrenchTestHome(),
15 );
16 }
17 }
```

Smaller reusable widgets help us to follow what is happening exactly.

That is also the advantage of stateless widgets. Unlike stateful widget, stateless widgets don't come with a huge boilerplate. Splitting code into smaller reusable code also makes it readable, which we cannot do with stateful widget.

In the view folder we've kept two more stateless widgets which will actually render the three controller widgets.

```
 1 import 'package:flutter/material.dart';
 2
 3 import 'french_test_first_view.dart';
 4
 5 class FrenchTestHome extends StatelessWidget {
 6 const FrenchTestHome({Key key}) : super(key: key);
 7
 8 @override
 9 Widget build(BuildContext context) {
10 return Scaffold(
11 appBar: AppBar(
12 title: Text('French Test'),
13 ),
14 body: FrenchTestFirstView(),
15 );
16 }
17 }
```

Since we have one page or screen, we'll identify the widget by name FrenchTestFirstView. And the code is like the following.

```
 1 import 'package:flutter/material.dart';
 2 import '../controller/first_row_widget.dart';
 3 import '../controller/second_row_widget.dart';
 4 import '../controller/third_row_widget.dart';
 5
 6 class FrenchTestFirstView extends StatelessWidget {
 7 const FrenchTestFirstView({Key key}) : super(key: key);
 8
 9 @override
10 Widget build(BuildContext context) {
11 return Center(
12 child: Column(
13 children: [
14 FirstRowWidget(),
15 SecondRowWidget(),
16 ThirdRowWidget(),
17 ],
18 ),
19 );
20 }
21 }
```

We've successfully split the long widget tree into smaller reusable widgets.

And our code is functioning perfectly reducing the widget rebuilds process.

15. Riverpod, a better Provider for state management

Riverpod is a provider, but different. If this statement doesn't make any sense, then please read on.

Riverpod is another state-management package library. Just like Provider.

We've already seen how to use the most popular flutter package, Provider, for state management. Now we're going to learn Riverpod to manage Flutter state in a better way.

Why do we need Riverpod? Provider is not bad either!

Yes, that's true. We have shown earlier how Provider state management package reduces widget-rebuilds.

However, in Flutter community, developers started complaining that provider package had some limitations. One of them, provider is not compile safe.

And another insufficiency was dependency injection. And all of these limitations came for one reason. The provider package depends on Flutter framework. It is a wrapper class of inherited widget.

So, the answer is Riverpod - the response to all the limitations of state management packages for Dart and Flutter apps.

Moreover, the new state management package, Riverpod, created by the same person Remi Rousselet, is also easy to maintain, test, and much less error-prone.

Riverpod has many options

Unlike provider, Riverpod state management package has too many choices. When you have too many good food on your table, it becomes difficult to choose the best one!

You need to choose from any of them.

```
1 Provider
2
3 StateProvider
4
5 StateNotifierProvider
6
7 ChangeNotifierProvider
8
9 StreamProvider
```

```
10
11 FutureProvider
12
13 ScopedProvider
```

From this list of options, we will always choose one according to our need. That means, one option is always the best for one specific problem.

We'll come to that point later. In this chapter. Because it needs a very detailed introspection.

As an example, when we want to watch or fetch a data from our model class we can use the simplest Provider from Riverpod package.

Now, we are going to learn how to use the simplest Provider from the Riverpod package.

Just to make this chapter more interesting we will use our old friend, the Provider state management package, also. In fact, you can always use two packages side by side.

The greatest advantage of Riverpod

As I have just said, there are too many options that come with Riverpod.

However, one of the greatest advantages is Riverpod helps us find the programming errors at compile time rather than at runtime.

What we have seen before?

An ugly Provider Not Found pops up soemtimes. This error is no more there. It's a great freedom indeed.

To start with we should add these dependencies in our pubspec.yaml file.

```
1 dependencies:
2 flutter:
3 sdk: flutter
4 flutter_riverpod:
5 provider:
```

We've not mentioned the version so that the packages can depend on the latest one available.

Let us see how our small app looks like.

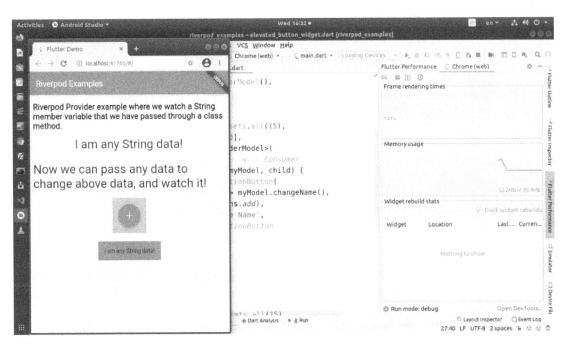

Figure 15.1 â€" Flutter Riverpod example

Just like our previous Provider chapter, we have used a model class for this Riverpod starter.

The Data Model on which we'll work in Riverpod

As you see in the above image, there is one class member variable, a String type. Below that we have a method through which we will pass any string value and we can watch it on the screen.

The floating action button below will change the string data below.

For the floating action event part we've used our old Provider package, not Riverpod. Because with the help of Riverpod Provider we will only watch the value.

Here is the model class:

```
 1 import 'package:flutter/widgets.dart';
 2 import 'package:flutter_riverpod/flutter_riverpod.dart';
 3
 4 class ProviderModel extends ChangeNotifier {
 5 String _littleMonk = 'I am any String data!';
 6 String get littleMonk => _littleMonk;
 7
 8 String fetchName(String str) {
 9 _littleMonk = str;
10 return _littleMonk;
11 }
12
13 void changeName() {
14 _littleMonk = 'Now I am Little Monk';
```

```
15 notifyListeners();
16 }
17 }
18
19 final classTypeProviderModel = Provider<ProviderModel>((ref) {
20 return ProviderModel();
21 });
```

Riverpod makes it really simple, because we can return the whole model class like this:

```
1 final classTypeProviderModel = Provider<ProviderModel>((ref) {
2 return ProviderModel();
3 });
```

Now, we can use "classTypeProviderModel" anywhere in our app, however large it is. As we have earlier said, Riverpod is Flutter independent.

In the above code, the "ref" parameter is of type ProviderReference. We'll see how we can use it to resolve dependencies between providers.

We need to understand that Provider object is now globally accessible. Here the "provided" object is ProviderModel class that has one state and some methods to change that state.

However, it does not mean that the provided object is now globally accessible.

Of course, like any other global function we can call it from anywhere. But we can also restrict the return value by scoping it locally.

Understanding Riverpod Scope

Now we will use this value provided by the Provider object inside different widget tree. Although Riverpod is Flutter independent, but in Flutter everything is widget!

Let us see the entry point of our app first.

```
1 import 'package:flutter/material.dart';
2 import 'package:flutter_riverpod/flutter_riverpod.dart';
3 import 'provider/controller/provider_example_widget.dart';
4
5 void main() {
6 runApp(ProviderScope(child: App()));
7 }
8
9 class App extends StatelessWidget {
10 // This widget is the root of your application.
11 @override
12 Widget build(BuildContext context) {
13 return MaterialApp(
14 title: 'Flutter Demo',
```

```
15 theme: ThemeData(
16 primarySwatch: Colors.blue,
17 ),
18 home: Home(),
19 );
20 }
21 }
22
23 class Home extends StatelessWidget {
24 const Home({Key key}) : super(key: key);
25
26 @override
27 Widget build(BuildContext context) {
28 return Container(
29 child: Scaffold(
30 appBar: AppBar(
31 title: Text('Riverpod Examples'),
32 ),
33 body: ProviderExampleWidget(),
34 ),
35 );
36 }
37 }
```

Please watch this part first:

```
1 void main() {
2 runApp(ProviderScope(child: App()));
3 }
```

It means the Riverpod package uses just one, yes, a single InheritedWidget. And we should place it above the whole widget tree.

I'm not going to detail how it can store state of all Provider objects. But we can use them anywhere.

How to watch a Provider object in Riverpod?

We can watch it by using Consumer builder like the following code snippet:

```
 1 import 'package:flutter/material.dart';
 2 import 'package:flutter_riverpod/flutter_riverpod.dart';
 3 //import 'package:provider/provider.dart';
 4 import '../model/any_type_provider_model.dart';
 5
 6 class ProviderExampleWidget extends StatelessWidget {
 7 const ProviderExampleWidget({Key key}) : super(key: key);
 8
 9 @override
10 Widget build(BuildContext context) {
11 return Column(
```

```
12 children: [
13 SizedBox(
14 height: 10.0,
15 ),
16 Padding(
17 padding: const EdgeInsets.all(18.0),
18 child: Text(
19 'Riverpod Provider example where we watch a String member variable'
20 ' that we have passed through a class method.',
21 style: TextStyle(
22 fontSize: 20.0,
23 fontWeight: FontWeight.bold,
24 ),
25 ),
26 ),
27 Padding(
28 padding: const EdgeInsets.all(18.0),
29 child: Center(
30 child: Consumer(
31 builder: (context, watch, child) {
32 final x = watch(classTypeProviderModel);
33 return Text(
34 x.fetchName('We can now pass any string data...'),
35 style: TextStyle(
36 fontSize: 50.0,
37 ),
38 );
39 },
40 ),
41 ),
42 ),
43 SizedBox(
44 height: 10.0,
45 ),
46 ],
47 );
48 }
49 }
```

In the above code this part holds the trick:

```
1 Consumer(
2 builder: (context, watch, child) {
3 final x = watch(classTypeProviderModel);
4 return Text(
5 x.fetchName('We can now pass any string data...'),
6 style: TextStyle(
7 fontSize: 50.0,
8 ),
9 );
```

```
10 },
11 ),
```

We'll show you a simpler method in a minute. That will drastically reduce the boilerplate code.

However, the above method reduces the widget rebuilds more than any other method. Here the Text widget is only rebuilt.

In the next code snippet we will see how we can pass "ScopedReader watch" through build() method and drastically reduce the boilerplate code.

How we can mix Riverpod Provider with old Provider package?

We're doing this just for fun! After all, coding is fun as long as you enjoy doing something new from nowhere!

In this app structure we have a controller folder as usual. As I always maintain the model-view-controller pattern.

You'll get the full code in this GitHub repository: The Riverpod all code repository for this book

In the controller folder, we have two widgets.

The first one will use "ScopedReader watch" as I've just mentioned.

```
1 import 'package:flutter/material.dart';
2 import 'package:flutter_riverpod/flutter_riverpod.dart';
3 import 'elevated_button_widget.dart';
4 import '../model/any_type_provider_model.dart';
5
6 class ProviderExampleWidget extends ConsumerWidget {
7 const ProviderExampleWidget({Key key}) : super(key: key);
8
9 @override
10 Widget build(BuildContext context, ScopedReader watch) {
11 final littleMonk = watch(classTypeProviderModel);
12 return Column(
13 children: [
14 SizedBox(
15 height: 10.0,
16 ),
17 Padding(
18 padding: const EdgeInsets.all(8.0),
19 child: Text(
20 'Riverpod Provider example where we watch a String member variable'
21 ' that we have passed through a class method.',
22 style: TextStyle(
23 fontSize: 20.0,
24 fontWeight: FontWeight.bold,
```

```
25 ),
26 ),
27 ),
28 Center(
29 child: Padding(
30 padding: const EdgeInsets.all(8.0),
31 child: Text(
32 littleMonk.littleMonk,
33 style: TextStyle(fontSize: 30.0),
34 ),
35 ),
36 ),
37 SizedBox(
38 height: 10.0,
39 ),
40 Center(
41 child: Padding(
42 padding: const EdgeInsets.all(8.0),
43 child: Text(
44 littleMonk
45 .fetchName('Now we can pass any data to change above data,'
46 ' and watch it!'),
47 style: TextStyle(fontSize: 30.0),
48 ),
49 ),
50 ),
51 SizedBox(
52 height: 10.0,
53 ),
54 ElevatedButtonWidget(),
55 ],
56 );
57 }
58 }
```

Now we can watch the Riverpod Provider object in a simpler way than before.

To do that we need a local object inside the build() method.

```
1 final littleMonk = watch(classTypeProviderModel);
```

After that watching Provided object becomes much simpler.

Now, we can easily access the model class member state like this:

```
1 Text(
2 littleMonk.littleMonk,
3 style: TextStyle(fontSize: 30.0),
4 ),
```

We can also change the state by passing a string data like this:

```
1 Text(
2 littleMonk
3 .fetchName('Now we can pass any data to change above data,'
4 ' and watch it!'),
5 style: TextStyle(fontSize: 30.0),
6 ),
```

However, we can also change the above provided object state by using our old Provider package and mix it with the Riverpod.

To do that we have used another custom widget and keep it inside the controller folder.

```
1 ElevatedButtonWidget(),
```

Let us see how we can now use the old Provider package to change the provided object state by pressing a button.

The old Provider package is really gold!

Yes, that's true. we have enough freedom to choose from any available options. We prefer the ChangeNotifierProvider<T> widget and return the Consumer<T> widgets just like before.

```
1 import 'package:flutter/material.dart';
2 import 'package:provider/provider.dart';
3 import '../model/any_type_provider_model.dart';
4
5 class ElevatedButtonWidget extends StatelessWidget {
6 const ElevatedButtonWidget({
7 Key key,
8 }) : super(key: key);
9
10 @override
11 Widget build(BuildContext context) {
12
13 return ChangeNotifierProvider<ProviderModel>(
14 // <--- ChangeNotifierProvider
15 create: (context) => ProviderModel(),
16 child: Column(
17 children: [
18 Container(
19 padding: const EdgeInsets.all(15),
20 color: Colors.blue[200],
21 child: Consumer<ProviderModel>(
22 // <--- Consumer
23 builder: (context, myModel, child) {
24 return FloatingActionButton(
25 onPressed: () => myModel.changeName(),
26 child: Icon(Icons.add),
27 tooltip: 'Change Name',
```

```
28 );
29 },
30 ),
31 ),
32 SizedBox(
33 height: 20.0,
34 ),
35 Container(
36 padding: const EdgeInsets.all(15),
37 color: Colors.redAccent,
38 child: Consumer<ProviderModel>(
39 // <--- Consumer
40 builder: (context, myModel, child) {
41 return Text(myModel.littleMonk);
42 },
43 ),
44 ),
45 ],
46 ),
47 );
48 }
49 }
```

Let's take a look at the image below, so we can understand how the whole structure reduces the widget-rebuilds.

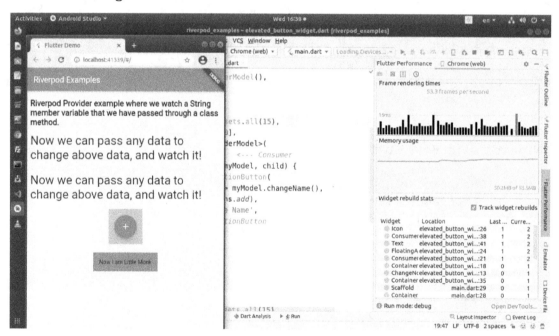

Figure 15.2 â€" Mixing Flutter Riverpod and old Provider package

Riverpod Provider and the old Provider package reduce the widget rebuilds

As we have pressed the button the It changes the state of the provided object globally. However, as you can see the locally scoped data state has not been affected at all.

As we've tracked the widget rebuilds we can also see that on the right hand side the statistics show how it benefits our app by reducing widget rebuilds.

When we've clicked the button, it only affects our custom ElevatedButtonWidget() widget.

For more Flutter related Articles and Resources

16. Riverpod ChangeNotifierProvider Widget and why it is important to autodispose

Our Riverpod series continues and in the last chapter, where we have discusses only Riverpod Provider, we've seen the most important part of the Riverpod state management.

Before reading this chapter, you must check the Provider part of Riverpod discussed in the last chapter.

In the last article we have mixed Riverpod and the old Provider package to have some coding fun. We've also checked how we can reduce widget rebuilds.

If you're already familiar with the Provider state management package, you must have used ChangeNotifierProvider already.

In fact, in this book, we have discussed Provider ChangeNotifierProvider in a great detail.

The new Riverpod state management package also uses the same ChangeNotifierProvider, but with a certain flavor, making it more advanced.

What does that mean?

For more Flutter related Articles and Resources

ChangeNotifierProvider in Provider package

Well, let us summarize and state again the main points of the ChangeNotifierProvider in Provider package first.

So you can associate these two features of Flutter state management quite easily.

We have seen use caes in our early examples. A model class that extends ChangeNotifier, can call notifyListeners() any time when the state in that class changed or updated.

In a model-view-controller pattern, usually in the view folder we notify the UI to rebuild the layout as our data gets updated.

And that is done through ChangeNotifierProvider.

ChangeNotifierProvider in Provider package is a kind of provider that provides the updated state object to any place in the UI layout.

If we've already used ChangeNotifier, in that case, it becomes much easier for us than before. Now we can do the same thing with the help of ChangeNotifierProvider and the Consumer widgets.

But in Riverpod the role of ChangeNotifierProvider has changed completely.

In Riverpod, ChangeNotifierProvider not only helps us to reduce widget rebuilds, but also it helps us to autodispose.

What is autodispose and why it is important?

The main concept is to destroy the state of a provider when it is no longer used.

Does ChangeNotifierProvider in Riverpod comes with the autodispose feature?

Yes, indeed! And that is the greatest advantage of ChangeNotifierProvider in Riverpod. And that is the main difference also with the ChangeNotifierProvider in old Provider package.

We'll see this difference in a minute, before that we must take a brief look at why autodispose is important?

There are multiple reasons for using this autodispose method that ChangeNotifierProvider in Riverpod comes with.

The main advantage is:

```
1 The first reason is, when using Firebase, to close the connection and
avoid unnecess\
2 ary cost is really important.
3
4 To reset the state when the user leaves a screen, go to another page
and re-enters i\
5 t.
```

We've learned a key concept, why ChangeNotifierProvider in Riverpod is different from the old ChangeNotifierProvider in Provider package.

In Provider package, the role of ChangeNotifierProvider was to provide an instance of a ChangeNotifier to its descendants.

Since it is a widget, it can have many descendants and we can directly sends the updated data to the bottom-most widget, without rebuilding the widget tree.

However, in Riverpod, the whole scenario takes a different route. Not only it helps us to auto-dispose, but it also simplifies the whole experience.

To demostrate the advantage of ChangeNotifierProvider in Riverpod we are going to make a simple app where we can add as many strings as we want with the help of pressing the button.

Now, in future, when we'll build an E-Commerce Flutter app we'll apply the same logic to add items to cart.

Let us see the image first. So we can have a clear picture.

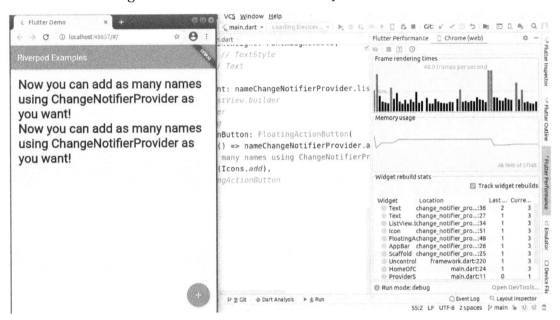

Figure 16.1 – ChangeNotifierProvider widget in Riverpod and autodispose

Since we have not used the typical model-view-controller pattern this time, this ChangeNotifierProvider has a large descendants.

Still the right hand side panel shows us how it helps us reduce the widget rebuilds.

Of course while building app, we would certainly avoid this process. We'll make our Flutter app structure more loosely coupled.

The entry point of ChangeNotifierProvider

It's our main method, this time we haven't used the ProviderScope to make it look simple.

```
1 import 'package:flutter/material.dart';
2 import 'package:flutter_riverpod/flutter_riverpod.dart';
3 import 'package:riverpod_examples/change-notifier-
provider/change_notifier_provider.\
4 dart';
5 import 'package:riverpod_examples/state-notifier-
```

```
provider/state_notifier_provider.da\
 6 rt';
 7
 8 import 'state-provider/view/state_provider_example.dart';
 9
10 void main() {
11 runApp(ProviderScope(child: App()));
12 }
13
14 class App extends StatelessWidget {
15 // This widget is the root of your application.
16 @override
17 Widget build(BuildContext context) {
18 return MaterialApp(
19 title: 'Flutter Demo',
20 theme: ThemeData(
21 primarySwatch: Colors.blue,
22 home: HomeOfChangeNotifierProvider(),
23 );
24 }
25 }
```

The model class and ChangeNotifier

Now we can define our model class that extends ChangeNotifier.

```
 1 import 'package:flutter/material.dart';
 2 import 'package:flutter/widgets.dart';
 3 import 'package:flutter_riverpod/flutter_riverpod.dart';
 4
 5 class NameNotifier extends ChangeNotifier {
 6 final List<String> listOfNames = [];
 7
 8 void addNames(String names) {
 9 listOfNames.add(names);
10 notifyListeners();
11 }
12 }
13
14 final nameChangeNotifier =
ChangeNotifierProvider.autoDispose<NameNotifier>((ref) {
15 return NameNotifier();
16 });
```

Nothing very exquisite. Except that we have used this line:

```
1 final nameChangeNotifier =
ChangeNotifierProvider.autoDispose<NameNotifier>((ref) {
2 return NameNotifier();
3 });
```

The rest part we have seen in our Provider package also.

That is our main challenge. We should be able to access that state object in multiple locations. At the same time we need to keep in our mind that we should structure our app in a way, so that it reduces widget rebuilds.

Now the syntax becomes much simpler than before. We can easily combine this object with others.

Like any other provider the ChangeNotifierProvider ensures one thing. The widget that reflects the updated data only gets recomputed.

```
 1 class HomeOfChangeNotifierProvider extends ConsumerWidget {
 2 const HomeOfChangeNotifierProvider({Key key}) : super(key: key);
 3
 4 @override
 5 Widget build(BuildContext context, ScopedReader watch) {
 6 final nameChangeNotifierProvider = watch(nameChangeNotifier);
 7
 8 return Scaffold(
 9 appBar: AppBar(
10 title: Text('Riverpod Examples'),
11 ),
12 body: Padding(
13 padding: const EdgeInsets.all(18.0),
14 child: Center(
15 child: ListView.builder(
16 itemBuilder: (context, index) {
17 return Text(
18 nameChangeNotifierProvider.listOfNames[index].toString(),
19 style: TextStyle(
20 fontSize: 30.0,
21 fontWeight: FontWeight.bold,
22 ),
23 );
24 },
25 itemCount: nameChangeNotifierProvider.listOfNames.length,
26 ),
27 ),
28 ),
29 floatingActionButton: FloatingActionButton(
30 onPressed: () => nameChangeNotifierProvider.addNames('Now you can '
31 'add as many names using ChangeNotifierProvider as you want!'),
32 child: Icon(Icons.add),
33 ),
34 );
35 }
36 }
```

Let's see how state management becomes much more easier than before with less boilerplate code.

```
1 Widget build(BuildContext context, ScopedReader watch) {
2 final nameChangeNotifierProvider = watch(nameChangeNotifier);
3
4 ...
```

Once we start watching, we can use ListView.builder() to show the items.

And adding items also becomes easier than before.

```
1 floatingActionButton: FloatingActionButton(
2 onPressed: () => nameChangeNotifierProvider.addNames('Now you can '
3 'add as many names using ChangeNotifierProvider as you want!'),
4 child: Icon(Icons.add),
5 ),
```

If you compare this ChangeNotifierProvider with the last chapter where we have discussed the Provider of Riverpod, you can realize that we can use Riverpod Provider in many ways.

In the next chapter we'll dig deep into StateProvider in Riverpod, another Provider variant of Riverpod.

For more Flutter related Articles and Resources

17. StateProvider in Riverpod, another Provider variant that makes State Management Simple

Let me clear the difference first. So you need not confuse between StateProvider in Riverpod and StateProvider in AngularJS. However the name is same.

What does distinguish them?

For that you need to know what StateProvider means in AngularJs first. After that, we will discuss this Provider variant in Flutter Riverpod. Moreover, we'll also try to build a Flutter app that will use StateProvider that provides different types of objects.

Although you're aware that Riverpod is a state management package in Flutter, still with reference to that, we've seen before how Provider package works in Flutter.

In AngularJs, Angular-UI-Router has stateProvider method which is used to create routes/states in application. However, in Riverpod state management package for Flutter, the role of StateProvider is completely different.

For more Flutter related Articles and Resources

What is StateProvider in Riverpod?

Where is the main difference that marks StateProvider in Riverpod special?

Riverpod has many Provider variants. As a result, you can use any one of them and get the same result. Certainly Provider is the most important component in Riverpod to manage state and autodispose the state object, all the same StateProvider has all characteristics we need.

The greatest advantage is of course, it reduces the widget rebuilds. But that too depends on how you plan the architecture of the app.

The Flutter app, we're going to build, will three different segments.

App structure and segments

The segment One is a very simple counter where you can press a floating action button and raise the number. In this case, the state object is an integer that will update its state using StateProvider.

In the second segment, as you scroll down the app, you will find four elevated buttons. The first button in the first row will change the name. The second button in the first row will change the city.

Just below that row we have second row, where we have again a first button that changes the name back to the previous one. And the second button in the second row will change the name and replaces the city name with the previous name.

They all are String objects, as in Dart everything is an object. The state object takes the String value, and with the press of buttons, it will change the state accordingly.

As we scroll down more, we'll find the third segment where the state object is a data model class. This class has two states. One is a String member variable and another is an Integer member variable. We'll change the state using class constructor.

StateProvider provides the state object

Firstly, to make this app we've extensively used only StateProvider. Secondly, we keep in mind that we can use same type of data twice.

However, there is one loophole in our app structure as long as widget rebuilds are concerned. Since we have many rows, we need to use VerticalDivider widget and to reduce the boilerplate code we had to extract that widget to a common widget.

Because it is unwise to use the same code and repeat them in places. However, that will backfire because the same widget gets rebuilt with the each press of button.

We'll track every widget rebuild so it gives us a clear idea how our app is working.

In this chapter of StateProvider, we will find the main difference in our data model.

In Riverpod we can have two providers expose a state of the same "type": We couldn't do that in package Provider.

To start with we'll first see how our Riverpod StateProvider app looks like:

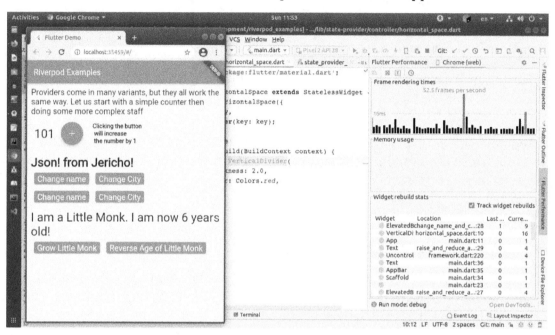

Figure 17.1 – Riverpod StateProvider Flutter app where we have pressed several buttons to change state of different StateProvider object. You can track the widget rebuilds on the right hand side.

I have just described this app above. It looks similar to the description having three separate segments. As we have used ListView widget as the top layout widget, so we could have added more below to scroll down safely.

Let us start with the entry point where we have our main method. Then we will discuss the code piece by piece.

```
 1 import 'package:flutter/material.dart';
 2 import 'package:flutter_riverpod/flutter_riverpod.dart';
 3 import 'package:riverpod_examples/change-notifier-
provider/change_notifier_provider.\
 4 dart';
 5 import 'package:riverpod_examples/state-notifier-
provider/state_notifier_provider.da\
 6 rt';
 7
 8 import 'state-provider/view/state_provider_example.dart';
 9
10 // import 'provider/controller/provider_example_widget.dart';
```

```
11
12 void main() {
13 runApp(ProviderScope(child: App()));
14 }
15
16 class App extends StatelessWidget {
17 // This widget is the root of your application.
18 @override
19 Widget build(BuildContext context) {
20 return MaterialApp(
21 title: 'Flutter Demo',
22 theme: ThemeData(
23 primarySwatch: Colors.blue,
24 ),
25 home: Home(),
26 );
27 }
28 }
29
30 class Home extends StatelessWidget {
31 const Home({Key key}) : super(key: key);
32
33 @override
34 Widget build(BuildContext context) {
35 return Scaffold(
36 appBar: AppBar(
37 title: Text('Riverpod Examples'),
38 ),
39
40 body: StateProviderExample(),
41 );
42 }
43 }
```

As you can see we have wrapped our Flutter app with ProviderScope(). Next important thing we have done is we've used two custom widgets to structure our app.

Although the widget tree starts with StateProviderExample() widget it returns a ListView widget, so we can build a UI that user can scroll.

The StateProviderExample() widget is the topmost widget in our layout UI widget tree.

The immediate descendant in the widget tree

Let us see the immediate descendant layout UI widget that is child to the StateProviderExample() widget.

```dart
1  import 'package:flutter/material.dart';
2  import 'package:flutter_riverpod/flutter_riverpod.dart';
3  import '../controller/change_name_and_city.dart';
4  import '../controller/clear_name_and_city.dart';
5  import '../controller/counter_widget.dart';
6  import '../controller/raise_and_reduce_age_of_little_monk.dart';
7  import '../controller/watch_name_and_city.dart';
8  import '../model/any_type_provider_model.dart';
9
10 class StateProviderExample extends ConsumerWidget {
11 const StateProviderExample({Key key}) : super(key: key);
12
13 @override
14 Widget build(BuildContext context, ScopedReader watch) {
15 final stateProviderIntegerObject =
   watch(stateProviderInteger).state;
16 final stateProviderNameObject = watch(stateProviderName).state;
17 final stateProviderCityObject = watch(stateProviderCity).state;
18 final stateProviderInstance = watch(stateProviderClass).state;
19
20 return Padding(
21 padding: EdgeInsets.all(
22 10.0,
23 ),
24 child: ListView(
25 children: [
26 Text(
27 'Providers come in many variants, but they all work the same way.'
28 ' Let us start with a simple counter then doing some more complex
   staff',
29 style: TextStyle(
30 fontSize: 20.0,
31 ),
32 ),
33 Padding(
34 padding: EdgeInsets.all(
35 8.0,
36 ),
37 child: CounterWidget(
38 stateProviderIntegerObject: stateProviderIntegerObject),
39 ),
40 Space(),
41 WatchNameAndCity(
42 stateProviderNameObject: stateProviderNameObject,
43 stateProviderCityObject: stateProviderCityObject),
44 ChangeNameAndCity(),
45 ClearNameAndCity(),
46 Space(),
47 Text(
48 '${stateProviderInstance.littleMonk}.'
```

```
49 ' I am now ${stateProviderInstance.ageOfLittleMonk} years old!',
50 style: TextStyle(
51 fontSize: 30.0,
52 ),
53 ),
54 RaiseAndReduceAgeOfLittleMonk(),
55 ],
56 ),
57 );
58 }
59 }
60
61 class Space extends StatelessWidget {
62 const Space({
63 Key key,
64 }) : super(key: key);
65
66 @override
67 Widget build(BuildContext context) {
68 return SizedBox(
69 height: 10.0,
70 );
71 }
72 }
```

As I was saying, the layout UI will showcase the controller widgets, and they come one after another. As a result inside the ListView widget children we place all controller widgets.

We know that the inside the controller widgets we will keep our business logic so that the data keeps coming from our models.

Therefore in the above code section, the following part is important as it shows how we have placed our controller widgets.

```
1 child: ListView(
2 children: [
3 Text(
4 'Providers come in many variants, but they all work the same way.'
5 ' Let us start with a simple counter then doing some more complex
staff',
6 style: TextStyle(
7 fontSize: 20.0,
8 ),
9 ),
10 Padding(
11 padding: EdgeInsets.all(
12 8.0,
```

```
13 ),
14 child: CounterWidget(
15 stateProviderIntegerObject: stateProviderIntegerObject),
16 ),
17 Space(),
18 WatchNameAndCity(
19 stateProviderNameObject: stateProviderNameObject,
20 stateProviderCityObject: stateProviderCityObject),
21 ChangeNameAndCity(),
22 ClearNameAndCity(),
23 Space(),
24 Text(
25 '${stateProviderInstance.littleMonk}.'
26 ' I am now ${stateProviderInstance.ageOfLittleMonk} years old!',
27 style: TextStyle(
28 fontSize: 30.0,
29 ),
30 ),
31 RaiseAndReduceAgeOfLittleMonk(),
32 ],
33 ),
```

By the way, at the top, we have our first custom widget CounterWidget that passes one StateProvider object. At any rate that should be an integer, and it happens to be that.

However, before we check the controller widgets separately, let us check the data model first.

The data model of StateProvider

The data model used in this flutter app, is not complex either. Now as regards StateProvider objects, we have defined four type of StateProvider objects that we have discussed earlier.

Mind you, in this data model, we have have two providers that expose a state of the same "type", that is String.

```
1 import 'package:flutter_riverpod/flutter_riverpod.dart';
2
3 final stateProviderInteger = StateProvider<int>((ref) {
4 return 100;
5 });
6
7 /// As opposed to when using package:provider,
8 /// in Riverpod we can have two providers expose a state of the same "type":
9 ///
10
11 final stateProviderName = StateProvider<String>((ref) {
```

```
12 return 'John';
13 });
14 final stateProviderCity = StateProvider<String>((ref) {
15 return 'Chicago';
16 });
17
18 class StateProviderModel {
19 String _littleMonk = '';
20 int _ageOfLittleMonk = 0;
21 String get littleMonk => _littleMonk;
22 int get ageOfLittleMonk => _ageOfLittleMonk;
23 StateProviderModel(this._littleMonk, this._ageOfLittleMonk);
24 }
25
26 final stateProviderClass = StateProvider<StateProviderModel>((ref) {
27 return new StateProviderModel('I am a Little Monk', 6);
28 });
```

We have two providers "stateProviderName" and "stateProviderCity", which expose the state of String type. To continue the same process, we could have done the same thing in our "StateProviderModel" class. However we've not done that. Instead we pass one String type and integer type through the class constructor.

How to read a StateProvider in Riverpod?

In my opinion, the following controller widget is the most important one where we have used the Riverpod read() to change the state of the provided objects.

```
1 import 'package:flutter/material.dart';
2 import 'package:flutter_riverpod/flutter_riverpod.dart';
3 import '../model/any_type_provider_model.dart';
4
5 void increment(BuildContext context) {
6 context.read(stateProviderInteger).state += 1;
7 }
8
9 void changeName(BuildContext context) {
10 context.read(stateProviderName).state = 'Json!';
11 }
12
13 void changeCity(BuildContext context) {
14 context.read(stateProviderCity).state = 'Jericho!';
15 }
16
17 void clearName(BuildContext context) {
18 context.read(stateProviderName).state = 'John';
19 }
20
21 void clearCity(BuildContext context) {
22 context.read(stateProviderCity).state = 'Chicago';
```

```
23 }
24
25 void changeLittleMonk(BuildContext context) {
26 context.read(stateProviderClass).state =
27 StateProviderModel('Now I am a big monk with white beard!', 70);
28 }
29
30 void reverseAgeOfLittleMonk(BuildContext context) {
31 context.read(stateProviderClass).state =
32 StateProviderModel('Now I am a little monk again!', 6);
33 }
```

We can clearly see that inside each method we have passed BuildConetxt context so the data flows through that context and we can read the Provider state.

The provider state object is either integer, or String, or even a data class. However in each case, the distinction is clear enough.

Because our app logic is clear, it's become easier for us to visualize what is going to happen.

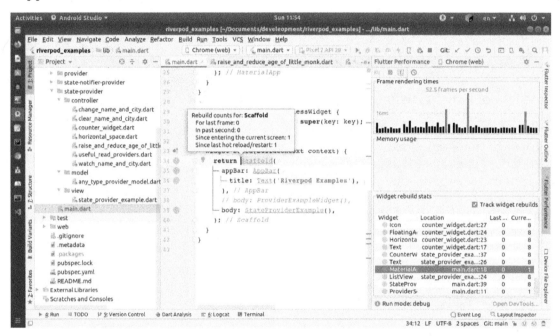

Figure 17.2 – Riverpod StateProvider Flutter app where we have pressed several buttons; however the Scaffold widget has not been rebuilt. You can track the widget rebuilds on the right hand side.

Now we can take a separate look at each controller widget where we have used used those earlier defined state properties and methods.

Since there are multiple ways to read the StateProvider, we will take the shortest route.

Now it entirely depends on you to which provider to listen and how will you do that. It also depends on the variant of Provider.There could be multiple possible values you want to listen to.

Anyway, since we have StateProvider and our first data model is an integer data object, first we have written it like this:

```
1 final stateProviderInteger = StateProvider<int>((ref) { return 100;
});
```

Then to read, we have defined the model method like this:

```
1 void increment(BuildContext context) {
context.read(stateProviderInteger).state += 1\
2 ; }
```

Now we can either watch() or read() that unchanged and changed state of the provided object.

We could have extended our controller widget to ConsumerWidget and passed ScopedReader watch object through the BuildContext() method. Or, we can just make our controller widget a child class of StatelessWidget and still can watch() read() the provided state object.

Take a look at our custom controller widget CounterWidget that extends the StatelessWidget and still can update the value.

```
 1 import 'package:flutter/material.dart';
 2 import 'useful_read_providers.dart';
 3 import 'horizontal_space.dart';
 4
 5 class CounterWidget extends StatelessWidget {
 6 const CounterWidget({
 7 Key key,
 8 @required this.stateProviderIntegerObject,
 9 }) : super(key: key);
10
11 final int stateProviderIntegerObject;
12
13 @override
14 Widget build(BuildContext context) {
15 return Row(
16 children: [
17 Text(
18 '${stateProviderIntegerObject.toString()}',
19 style: TextStyle(
```

```
20 fontSize: 30.0,
21 ),
22 ),
23 HorizontalSpace(),
24 FloatingActionButton(
25 onPressed: () => increment(context),
26 tooltip: 'Increment',
27 child: Icon(Icons.add),
28 ),
29 HorizontalSpace(),
30 Container(
31 padding: EdgeInsets.all(
32 8.0,
33 ),
34 child: Text(
35 'Clicking the button \n will increase \n the number by 1',
36 style: TextStyle(
37 fontSize: 15.0,
38 fontWeight: FontWeight.bold,
39 ),
40 ),
41 ),
42 ],
43 );
44 }
45 }
```

Does StateProvider look very complicated? On the contrary, it is extremely simple. The simplicity reflects on these two lines of code. The first one we have passed through the Text() widget and watch() the old and new updated value.

```
1 '${stateProviderIntegerObject.toString()}',
```

The second one, that is the read() part is even simpler than the watch(). Is it true? Look at the one line of code that we used in floating action button.

```
1 onPressed: () => increment(context),
```

Now whatever time you press the floating action button to increment the counter value, it won't affect the parent widgets of the tree. So in all cases, the Scaffold() never gets rebuilt.

However, other related widgets have been rebuilt.

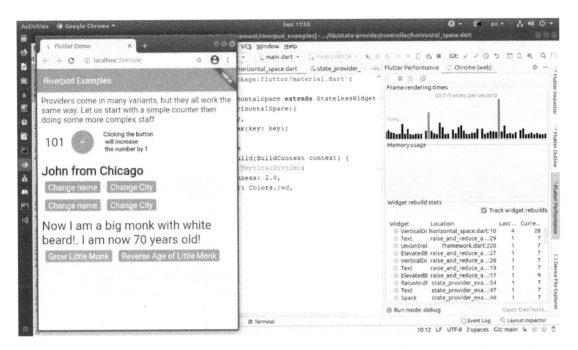

Figure 17.3 – Riverpod StateProvider Flutter app where we have pressed several buttons to change state of different StateProvider object. You can track the number of widget rebuilds on the right hand side.

Reading other StateProvider

By and large other controller widgets follow the same rule. Because we want multiple controller widgets to handle the changing the name and city, we have placed them in separate widgets.

The first one is as the following one:

```
1 import 'package:flutter/material.dart';
2 import 'horizontal_space.dart';
3 import 'useful_read_providers.dart';
4
5 class ChangeNameAndCity extends StatelessWidget {
6 const ChangeNameAndCity({
7 Key key,
8 }) : super(key: key);
9
10 @override
11 Widget build(BuildContext context) {
12 return Padding(
13 padding: EdgeInsets.all(
14 8.0,
15 ),
16 child: Row(
17 children: [
18 ElevatedButton(
19 onPressed: () => changeName(context),
```

```
20 child: Text(
21 'Change name',
22 style: TextStyle(
23 fontSize: 20.0,
24 ),
25 ),
26 ),
27 HorizontalSpace(),
28 ElevatedButton(
29 onPressed: () => changeCity(context),
30 child: Text(
31 'Change City',
32 style: TextStyle(
33 fontSize: 20.0,
34 ),
35 ),
36 ),
37 ],
38 ),
39 );
40 }
41 }
```

To start with we have to change the name and after that we have to change the city. And everything gets done by pressing the consecutive buttons.

How to get back the previous name and city?

However, at the same time, we want to get back the old name and city. So we need to have another controller widget for that.

```
1 import 'package:flutter/material.dart';
2 import 'horizontal_space.dart';
3 import 'useful_read_providers.dart';
4
5 class ClearNameAndCity extends StatelessWidget {
6 const ClearNameAndCity({
7 Key key,
8 }) : super(key: key);
9
10 @override
11 Widget build(BuildContext context) {
12 return Padding(
13 padding: EdgeInsets.all(
14 8.0,
15 ),
16 child: Row(
17 children: [
18 ElevatedButton(
19 onPressed: () => clearName(context),
```

```
20 child: Text(
21 'Change name',
22 style: TextStyle(
23 fontSize: 20.0,
24 ),
25 ),
26 ),
27 HorizontalSpace(),
28 ElevatedButton(
29 onPressed: () => clearCity(context),
30 child: Text(
31 'Change City',
32 style: TextStyle(
33 fontSize: 20.0,
34 ),
35 ),
36 ),
37 ],
38 ),
39 );
40 }
41 }
```

On top of that, at the same time we need to place the name and city side by side through another custom widget. As a result, one button-press changes the String data object.

Watching the StateProvider

Although the code snippet is shorter than the other, still it plays the important role as it watches the provider.

```
1 import 'package:flutter/material.dart';
2
3 class WatchNameAndCity extends StatelessWidget {
4 const WatchNameAndCity({
5 Key key,
6 @required this.stateProviderNameObject,
7 @required this.stateProviderCityObject,
8 }) : super(key: key);
9
10 final String stateProviderNameObject;
11 final String stateProviderCityObject;
12
13 @override
14 Widget build(BuildContext context) {
15 return Text(
16 stateProviderNameObject + ' from ' + stateProviderCityObject,
17 style: TextStyle(
18 fontSize: 30.0,
```

```
19 fontWeight: FontWeight.bold,
20 ),
21 );
22 }
23 }
```

Certainly for the absolute beginners this process of breaking down the whole app architecture seems daunting, but it is necessary. Moreover, it makes our code testable, produces less boilerplate code.

Now as regards the less boilerplate, the Riverpod state management makes a huge difference.

Why so? Because now we can place our Provider watch() and read() in our controller folder and call them as necessary.

Watch and Read the final StateProvider of our Flutter app

Now we are going to build the third and the final segment of our app. In doing that we need to take a close look at these watch() and read() part of our business logic first.

In our data model we have defined the Provider state object as a class.

```
 1 class StateProviderModel {
 2 String _littleMonk = '';
 3 int _ageOfLittleMonk = 0;
 4 String get littleMonk => _littleMonk;
 5 int get ageOfLittleMonk => _ageOfLittleMonk;
 6 StateProviderModel(this._littleMonk, this._ageOfLittleMonk);
 7 }
 8
 9 final stateProviderClass = StateProvider<StateProviderModel>((ref) {
10 return new StateProviderModel('I am a Little Monk', 6);
11 });
```

Next, we read() the StateProvider object by adopting the following process:

```
1 void changeLittleMonk(BuildContext context) {
2 context.read(stateProviderClass).state =
3 StateProviderModel('Now I am a big monk with white beard!', 70);
4 }
5
6 void reverseAgeOfLittleMonk(BuildContext context) {
7 context.read(stateProviderClass).state =
8 StateProviderModel('Now I am a little monk again!', 6);
9 }
```

Consequently our task becomes easier now. And as a result, we can raise the age of little monk and reverse it back with an updated text message.

Model to Controller to View

To follow this pattern, we have kept a separate controller widget, which will change the state of the little monk.

```
1 import 'package:flutter/material.dart';
2 import 'useful_read_providers.dart';
3
4 class RaiseAndReduceAgeOfLittleMonk extends StatelessWidget {
5 const RaiseAndReduceAgeOfLittleMonk({
6 Key key,
7 }) : super(key: key);
8
9 @override
10 Widget build(BuildContext context) {
11 return Padding(
12 padding: EdgeInsets.all(
13 8.0,
14 ),
15 child: Row(
16 children: [
17 ElevatedButton(
18 onPressed: () => changeLittleMonk(context),
19 child: Text(
20 'Grow Little Monk',
21 style: TextStyle(
22 fontSize: 20.0,
23 ),
24 ),
25 ),
26 VerticalDivider(),
27 ElevatedButton(
28 onPressed: () => reverseAgeOfLittleMonk(context),
29 child: Text(
30 'Reverse Age of Little Monk',
31 style: TextStyle(
32 fontSize: 20.0,
33 ),
34 ),
35 ),
36 ],
37 ),
38 );
39 }
40 }
```

Firstly, the context plays the key role throughout this app. Secondly we need to pass that context through the method we've defined.

For instance, these two following methods complete our task.

```
1 onPressed: () => changeLittleMonk(context),
2
3 onPressed: () => reverseAgeOfLittleMonk(context),
```

No doubt, not only it reduces the widget rebuilds, but at the same time, it also makes less boilerplate.

The only chink in our Flutter app's armor

It's a good practice that you break your spaghetti code in separate modules. However, sometimes it may backfire. Consequently it unnecessarily rebuilds one single widget again and again. It not only consumes memory, but it also slows down the app's performance.

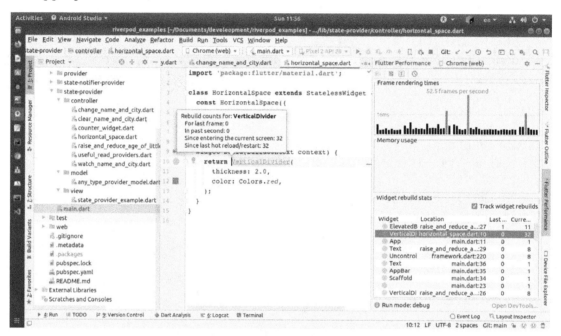

Figure 17.4 – Riverpod StateProvider Flutter app where we have pressed several buttons to change state of different StateProvider object and that affets VerticalDivider widget. It has been rebuilt 32 times. We could have avoided that. You can track the widget rebuilds on the right hand side.

On top of that, it does not make your flutter app performant enough.

What can we do?

We need to track the widget rebuilds while building our app. That is the first step. The second most important step is to rectify the fault.

For that reason we could have avoided the following extraction of a separate widget:

```
1 import 'package:flutter/material.dart';
2
3 class HorizontalSpace extends StatelessWidget {
4 const HorizontalSpace({
```

```
 5 Key key,
 6 }) : super(key: key);
 7
 8 @override
 9 Widget build(BuildContext context) {
10 return VerticalDivider(
11 thickness: 2.0,
12 color: Colors.red,
13 );
14 }
15 }
```

Instead we can use VerticalDivider widget where it is needed.

18. What is StateNotifier and StateNotifierProvider in Riverpod Flutter? How it reduces Widget Rebuilds?

StateNotifierProvider is just another Provider variant in Riverpod to manage state in Flutter. However, there is a remarkable difference with ChangeNotifierProvider.

The StateNotifierProvider does not use notifyListener() any more as it does not extend the data model with ChangeNotifier. However it depends on StateNotifier, a flutter independent mutable state change mechanism that has similirity with ChangeNotifier or ValueNotifier.

We'll come to that point and discuss the core concepts in detail in the later part of this chapter.

So, stay tuned and read on.

In our previous chapter 16, we have seen how ChangeNotifierProvider extends ChangeNotifier from Flutter and notify listeners.

In such cases, the subscribers listen to the notification and update the state accordingly.

Instead, the StateNotifierProvider extends the data model with StateNotifier, which operates with a certain type, and this type could be a very simple primitive data type, such as integer, or it could be quite complex like any user defined abstract class that has many children.

However, in the first part of this chapter we keep things very simple so you can have an idea about how StateNotifierProvider works with StateNotifier.

Since the data model of StateNotifierProvider extends StateNotifier, it looks different from other Provider variant of Riverpod state management package in Flutter.

Although the functionality is the same, it works on a different principle.

Let's take a look at the data model first.

```
1 class NameNotifier extends StateNotifier<List<String>> {
2 NameNotifier() : super([]);
3 void addNames(String names) {
4 state = [...state, names];
5 }
6
7 void deleteNames(String names) {
8 state = [
9 for (final loopNames in state)
10 if (names != loopNames) loopNames,
11 ];
12 }
13 }
14
15 final nameNotifierProvider =
StateNotifierProvider<NameNotifier>((ref) {
16 return NameNotifier();
17 });
```

Either you can place this data model in a separate model folder or you can use it with the main UI layout.

Whatever we do, when we run this simple app, it looks like this:

Figure 18.1 â€" A simple flutter app using StateNotifierProvider in Riverpod

As we press the floating action button, the String text is getting added one after another, just like the below image.

Figure 18.2 â€" Adding items using StateNotifierProvider in Riverpod

Now, we can track the widget rebuilds and watch the progress bar. We have pressed the button seven times. As a result, the Text widget that displays the provided String data object has been rebuilt 21 times.

Since we have placed everything under Scaffold() that widget was also rebuilt 7 times.

Let us see the main entry point of our small app, where we have returned the HomeStateNotifierProvider().

Next, we will define our layout UI in that custom widget later.

```
 1 import 'package:flutter/material.dart';
 2 import 'package:flutter_riverpod/flutter_riverpod.dart';
 3 import 'package:riverpod_examples/change-notifier-
provider/change_notifier_provider.\
 4 dart';
 5 import 'package:riverpod_examples/state-notifier-
provider/state_notifier_provider.da\
 6 rt';
 7
 8 import 'state-provider/view/state_provider_example.dart';
 9
10 void main() {
11 runApp(ProviderScope(child: App()));
12 }
13
14 class App extends StatelessWidget {
15 // This widget is the root of your application.
16 @override
17 Widget build(BuildContext context) {
18 return MaterialApp(
19 title: 'Flutter Demo',
20 theme: ThemeData(
21 primarySwatch: Colors.blue,
22 ),
23 home: HomeStateNotifierProvider(),
24 );
25 }
26 }
```

If we include the data model, the HomeStateNotifierProvider widget code snippet looks like this.

```
 1 import 'package:flutter/material.dart';
 2 import 'package:flutter/widgets.dart';
 3 import 'package:flutter_riverpod/flutter_riverpod.dart';
 4
 5 class NameNotifier extends StateNotifier<List<String>> {
 6 NameNotifier() : super([]);
 7 void addNames(String names) {
 8 state = [...state, names];
 9 }
```

```
10
11 void deleteNames(String names) {
12 state = [
13 for (final loopNames in state)
14 if (names != loopNames) loopNames,
15 ];
16 }
17 }
18
19 final nameNotifierProvider =
StateNotifierProvider<NameNotifier>((ref) {
20 return NameNotifier();
21 });
22
23 class HomeStateNotifierProvider extends ConsumerWidget {
24 const HomeStateNotifierProvider({Key key}) : super(key: key);
25
26 @override
27 Widget build(BuildContext context, ScopedReader watch) {
28 final nameStateNotifierProvider = watch(nameNotifierProvider.state);
29 return Scaffold(
30 appBar: AppBar(
31 title: Text('Riverpod Examples'),
32 ),
33
34 body: Padding(
35 padding: const EdgeInsets.all(18.0),
36 child: Center(
37 child: ListView.builder(
38 itemBuilder: (context, index) {
39 return Text(
40 nameStateNotifierProvider[index].toString(),
41 style: TextStyle(
42 fontSize: 30.0,
43 fontWeight: FontWeight.bold,
44 ),
45 );
46 },
47 itemCount: nameStateNotifierProvider.length,
48 ),
49 ),
50 ),
51 floatingActionButton: FloatingActionButton(
52 onPressed: () =>
53 context.read(nameNotifierProvider).addNames('Now you can '
54 'add as many names as you want!'),
55 child: Icon(Icons.add),
56 ),
57 );
```

```
58  }
59  }
```

Now we can run the app and add as many items as we want.

The advantage of Riverpod is it gives you enough freedom to choose from many options. If you compare them it looks like a difficult task.

However, keep one thing in mind, you will always choose the best Provider variant according to the nature of your app that you're going to build.

The relation between StateNotifierProvider and StateNotifier, a complex app structure

Since we're going to learn StateNotifierProvider in Riverpod Flutter, we first know what StateNotifier is.

However, they are not exactly the same. Although they depend on each other.

You may think of State Notifier as the Flutter independent state management component.

While State Notifier entirely revolves around one single property state, State Notifier Provider manages to provide that state.

State Notifier is just like mutable ChangeNotifier, which acts like Flutter default ValueNotifier.

With their help any widget can listen to the state, however Provider has to to provide that state.

State Notifier Provider is another Provider variant in Riverpod

That is where Riverpod StateNotifierProvider enters into the scene. Of course,it takes help from StateNotifier to provide the state that to a bottom-most widget that needs the state.

Now StateNotifier can either operate with a single primitive data type, like integer; or, it can handle a very complex user-defined data type.

Whatever, the nature of state, simple or complex, State Notifier Provider takes the child of State Notifier on its shoulder and carries the state to any widget that needs it.

And while doing so it considerably reduces the widget rebuilds.

How StateNotifierProvider reduces widget rebuilds?

The core concept of Riverpod spins round one main challenge. The challenge is to send the state property to the bottom-most widget without disturbing the widget hierarchy.

If the bottom-most widget has an expensive widget tree on the top and still it wants to listen to the state, two things can happen.

When we press a button to listen to the state in the bottom-most widget, the whole widget tree gets rebuilt. And that will be worst scenario. It happens in the case of stateful widget.

Of course, the best solution is something else. In that case, only the bottom-most widget gets rebuilt and everything on the top remains like before.

StateNotifierProvider with the help of StateNotifier does the same thing.

We're going to show it in a minute. Moreover, you can take a look at the image above where I have tried to demonstrate the whole app structure.

What does StateNotifierProvider in Riverpod mean?

If we break the word StateNotifierProvider into three parts, what we find? Three separate meaningful words.

State, Notifier and Provider.

As we know state is a built-in characteristic or property of an object. Like a person has name, height, weight, etc. Now a notifier needs to notify the change of state to a widget. However, to while notifying it must provide them.

Let us consider an app like this:

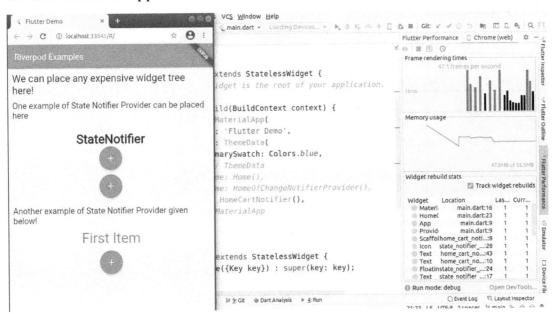

Figure 18.3 - A Flutter app uses StateNotifierProvider and track widget rebuilds

On the left hand side, we can see the app. And, on the right hand side, we can track the widget rebuilds.

Despite the fact that the app looks very simple, in reality the structure is not that simple.

Because we want to reduce widget rebuilds, we break the code in separate modules, making them loosely coupled.

What kind of state we need to notify and provide?

Granted, the nature of state is not simple always. But for this example we have kept both. Simple and complex.

A simple data model class that extends StateNotifier looks like this:

```
1 class NameNotifier extends StateNotifier<String> {
2 NameNotifier() : super('StateNotifier');
3
4 void addNames(String names) {
5 state = names;
6 }
7
8 void updateNames(String names) {
9 state = names;
10 }
11 }
12
13 final nameNotifierProvider =
StateNotifierProvider<NameNotifier>((ref) {
14 return NameNotifier();
15 });
```

In addition to the simplicity of the nature of the state here (it is String), StateNotifierProvider also acts in a simple way. It returns the state as a reference.

Now, any widget, anywhere in the widget tree, can listen to it.

Nevertheless the complex data model looks like the above.

```
1 class ClassOfItems {
2 String items;
3 ClassOfItems({this.items});
4 }
5
6 class CartNotifier extends StateNotifier<ClassOfItems> {
7 CartNotifier() : super(ClassOfItems(items: 'First Item'));
8 void addToCart(ClassOfItems items) {
9 state = items;
10 }
11 }
12
13 final itemNotifier = StateNotifierProvider<CartNotifier>((ref) {
```

```
14 return CartNotifier();
15 });
```

In the second data model, StateNotifier operates on a user defined type, which could have been more complex.

As we have two data models in model folders, we can think about creating the layout UI now. Next, we should place them in separate folders.

After that we will press every button to see how it affects the top widgets. Besides, we'll track the widget rebuilds of child widgets where we're listening to the state.

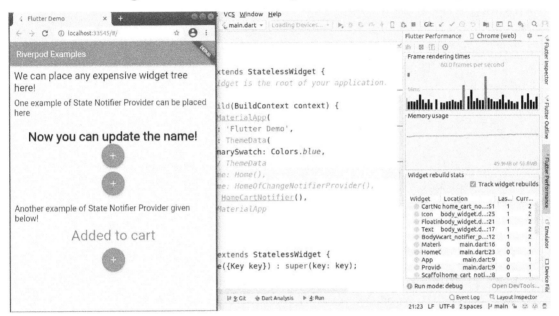

Figure 18.4 - Flutter app uses StateNotifierProvider and reduces widget rebuilds

The right hand side Flutter Performance statistics shows us how only child widgets has got rebuilt. On the other hand, this state changing process has not touched the top widgets.

The entry point and the model, view, controller

The main method calls a runApp() method and passes our App(), which returns HomeCartNotifier().

Why should we break our code in separate modules?

Because we don't want to rebuild the top widgets when the bottom-most widgets listen to the state.

Not only that, StateNotifierProvider also helps us to tackle the dependency injection, and compile time error in an efficient way. However, to make it happen, we need to plan our app structure in that way.

```
 1 void main() {
 2 runApp(ProviderScope(child: App()));
 3 }
 4
 5 class App extends StatelessWidget {
 6 // This widget is the root of your application.
 7 @override
 8 Widget build(BuildContext context) {
 9 return MaterialApp(
10 title: 'Flutter Demo',
11 theme: ThemeData(
12 primarySwatch: Colors.blue,
13 ),
14 // home: Home(),
15 // home: HomeOfChangeNotifierProvider(),
16 home: HomeCartNotifier(),
17 );
18 }
19 }
```

Consequently the HomeCartNotifier() again returns AnExpensiveWidget() that makes a long widget tree.

```
 1 class HomeCartNotifier extends StatelessWidget {
 2 @override
 3 Widget build(BuildContext context) {
 4 return Scaffold(
 5 appBar: AppBar(
 6 title: Text('Riverpod Examples'),
 7 ),
 8 body: AnExpensiveWidget(),
 9 );
10 }
11 }
```

Although the An Expensive Widget makes a long widget tree and a child of Scaffold widget, when we change the state, they will not be rebuilt.

Now we can take a look at the structure of An Expensive Widget.

More you break, your code becomes more readable and maintainable

An Expensive Widget uses a List View widget so we can scroll down if necessary. Moreover, there is another reason.

We can accommodate Column or Row layout widgets inside List View. There will be no UI conflict.

However, we need to be aware of not using this advantage too much in one single screen.

Instead we can use multiple screens to pass state.

Even though for this example we use one single screen, this is not the best practice. Well, let us see An Expensive Widget tree.

```
1 class AnExpensiveWidget extends StatelessWidget {
2 @override
3 Widget build(BuildContext context) {
4 return Padding(
5 padding: EdgeInsets.all(
6 10.0,
7 ),
8 child: ListView(
9 children: [
10 Text(
11 'We can place any expensive widget tree here!',
12 style: Theme.of(context).textTheme.headline5,
13 ),
14 SizedBox(
15 height: 10.0,
16 ),
17 Text(
18 'One example of State Notifier Provider'
19 ' can be placed here',
20 style: Theme.of(context).textTheme.headline6,
21 ),
22 SizedBox(
23 height: 10.0,
24 ),
25 class AnExpensiveWidget extends StatelessWidget {
26 @override
27 Widget build(BuildContext context) {
28 return Padding(
29 padding: EdgeInsets.all(
30 10.0,
31 ),
32 child: ListView(
33 children: [
34 Text(
35 'We can place any expensive widget tree here!',
36 style: Theme.of(context).textTheme.headline5,
37 ),
38 SizedBox(
39 height: 10.0,
40 ),
41 Text(
42 'One example of State Notifier Provider'
43 ' can be placed here',
44 style: Theme.of(context).textTheme.headline6,
45 ),
```

```
46 SizedBox(
47 height: 10.0,
48 ),
49 HomeStateNotifierProvider(),
50 // HomeStateNotifierProvider(),
51 Text(
52 'Another example of State Notifier Provider'
53 ' given below!',
54 style: Theme.of(context).textTheme.headline6,
55 ),
56 SizedBox(
57 height: 10.0,
58 ),
59 CartNotifierProvider(),
60 ],
61 ),
62 );
63 }
64 }
65 ,
66 Text(
67 'Another example of State Notifier Provider'
68 ' given below!',
69 style: Theme.of(context).textTheme.headline6,
70 ),
71 SizedBox(
72 height: 10.0,
73 ),
74 CartNotifierProvider(),
75 ],
76 ),
77 );
78 }
79 }
```

Now we have two child widgets. The first is HomeStateNotifierProvider that listens to NameNotifier state.

Another child widget is CartNotifierProvider, which listens to CartNotifier state.

As we progress we will see how these two child widgets only get rebuilt. And, as a result, that widget rebuilds will not affect the higher widgets.

How HomeStateNotifierProvider listens to NameNotifier

The HomeStateNotifierProvider extends the ConsumerWidget of Riverpod package and that helps to watch and read the StateNotifierProvider state property.

As a result, with the help of watch() and read() method we can view the state,as well as change the state.

```dart
1 class HomeStateNotifierProvider extends ConsumerWidget {
2 const HomeStateNotifierProvider({Key key}) : super(key: key);
3
4 @override
5 Widget build(BuildContext context, ScopedReader watch) {
6 final nameStateNotifierProvider = watch(nameNotifierProvider.state);
7 return Padding(
8 padding: const EdgeInsets.all(18.0),
9 child: Center(
10 child: Column(
11 children: [
12 Text(
13 nameStateNotifierProvider.toString(),
14 style: TextStyle(
15 fontSize: 30.0,
16 fontWeight: FontWeight.bold,
17 ),
18 ),
19 FloatingActionButton(
20 onPressed: () =>
21 context.read(nameNotifierProvider).addNames('Now you can '
22 'add name!'),
23 child: Icon(Icons.add),
24 ),
25 SizedBox(
26 height: 10.0,
27 ),
28 FloatingActionButton(
29 onPressed: () =>
30 context.read(nameNotifierProvider).updateNames('Now you can '
31 'update the name!'),
32 child: Icon(Icons.add),
33 ),
34 ],
35 ),
36 ),
37 );
38 }
39 }
```

As you can see, we've used two floating action buttons. One for adding names. And the other for updating the names.

How CartNotifierProvider listens to CartNotifier

Since the CartNotifier as a child of StateNotifier operates on a more complex state, we need to be careful.

Although that doesn't change the basic operation style. As always we've used Consumer Widget from Riverpod package. Besides we also use watch() and read() methods.

But there is only one change to make our code readable. Hence we use another custom widget that controls the operation.

```
1 class CartNotifierProvider extends ConsumerWidget {
2 const CartNotifierProvider({Key key}) : super(key: key);
3
4 @override
5 Widget build(BuildContext context, ScopedReader watch) {
6 final cartStateNotifierProvider = watch(itemNotifier.state);
7 return BodyWidget(cartStateNotifierProvider:
cartStateNotifierProvider);
8 }
9 }
```

When the return part of the above code is important you can guess we should keep that custom Body Widget inside the controller folder.

However, that enhances the readability of our code. And to maintain that readability we should document by adding comments at the appropriate position.

Moreover, we need to be careful about the dependency injection, since we've used it inside Body Widget.

```
 1 class BodyWidget extends StatelessWidget {
 2 const BodyWidget({
 3 Key key,
 4 @required this.cartStateNotifierProvider,
 5 }) : super(key: key);
 6
 7 final ClassOfItems cartStateNotifierProvider;
 8
 9 @override
10 Widget build(BuildContext context) {
11 return Center(
12 child: Column(children: [
13 Text(cartStateNotifierProvider.items,
14 style: Theme.of(context).textTheme.headline4,
15 ),
16 SizedBox(height: 10.0,),
17 FloatingActionButton(
18 onPressed: () => context.read(itemNotifier).addToCart(
19 ClassOfItems(items: 'Added to cart'),
20 ),
21 child: Icon(Icons.add),
22 ),
23 ],
24 ),
```

```
25 );
26 }
27 }
```

While we have done so many things to reduce widget rebuilds, has that worked really? Well, we have proof in our hand.

Since we have tracked the widget rebuilds at each step, we have solid evidence.

Look here at the below image, where it clearly shows the number of rebuilds of the Scaffold widget.

Remember, the same is true for the topmost widget App. Besides, it is also true for every descendant widgets that do not listen to the state.

Figure 18.5 - The topmost parent widget and its descendant widgets are not rebuilt as state changes

For more Flutter related Articles and Resources

19. Riverpod migration, WidgetRef ref, and What is new in Riverpod

To use Riverpod state management package in Flutter, we need to assure ourselves a few things first.

Firstly, we need to use Riverpod latest package: ^0.14.0.

Secondly, we must upgrade our Flutter and Dart SDK.

Finally, we need to migrate to latest Riverpod from [0.13.0. to]0.14.0.

In this chapter, we're going to see how we can successfully migrate from old Riverpod version to the newest version.

As regards to this tutorial, you may get the full code in this GitHub repository mentioned in the last chapter. And besides, if you want to dig deep into the flutter state management, you may read all updated Flutter articles in my website. For more Flutter related Articles and Resources

By the way, the above mentioned flutter app using Riverpod was built using Riverpod ^0.13.0. and that is not working anymore.

Therefore the only solution left to us is Riverpod migration.

To migrate successfully from the old Riverpod to the newest version, we need to install the migration tool, that is Riverpod command line interface.

```
1 dart pub global activate riverpod_cli
```

However, we need to change the path of the executables.

```
1 export PATH="$PATH":"$HOME/.pub-cache/bin"
```

Now, as a result, we can use Riverpod Command line interface.

```
1 riverpod --help
```

And it gives us the following output.

```
 1 Usage: riverpod <command> [arguments]
 2
 3 Global options:
 4 -h, --help    Print this usage information.
 5
 6 Available commands:
 7 migrate    Analyse a project using Riverpod and migrate it to the
latest version avai\
 8 lable
 9
10 Run "riverpod help <command>" for more information about a command.
11 ...
```

All right, now we are ready to migrate and it looks like the following screenshot.

```
14   final stateProviderCity = StateProvider<String>((ref) {
15     return 'Chicago';
16   });
17
```

Figure 19.1 – Riverpod Command line interface

Next, we need to migrate from old Riverpod to the new, by issuing the following command.

```
1 riverpod migrate
```

Consequently, it might display the following message depending on your project and ask your permission to go ahead.

```
1 Widget build(BuildContext context, ScopedReader watch) {
2 -   StateProviderModel state = watch(provider.state);
3 +   StateProviderModel state = watch(provider);
4 }
5
6 Accept change (y = yes, n = no [default], A = yes to all, q = quit)?
7 Let us accept the change and it looks like the following screenshot.
```

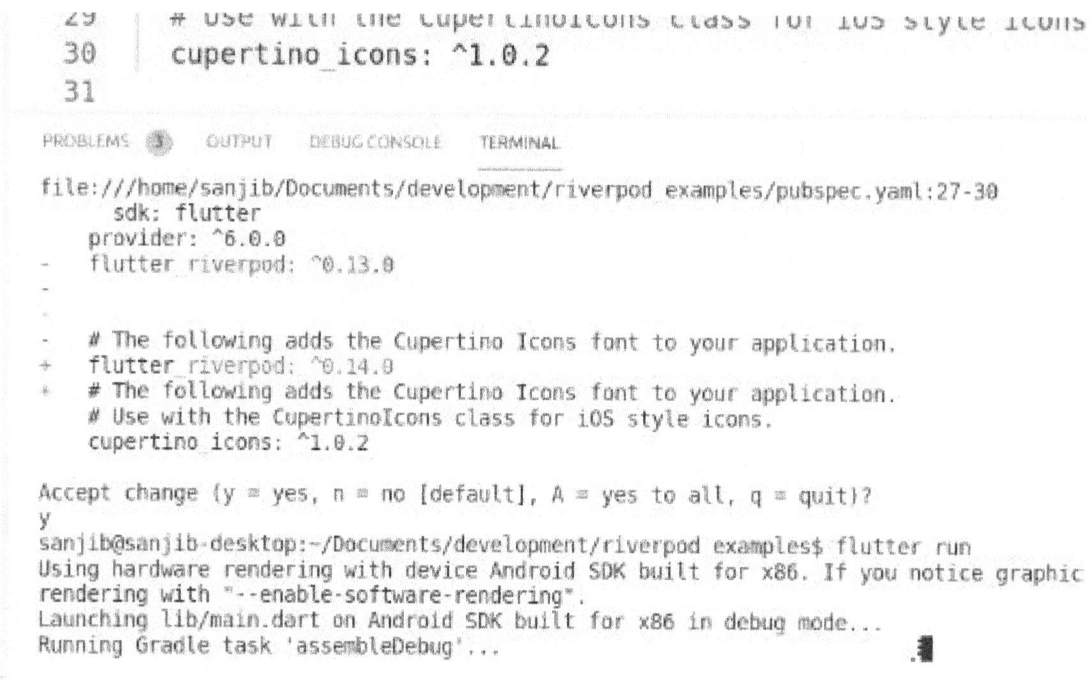

```
29      # Use with the CupertinoIcons class for iOS style icons
30      cupertino_icons: ^1.0.2
31
```

```
PROBLEMS 3    OUTPUT    DEBUG CONSOLE    TERMINAL

file:///home/sanjib/Documents/development/riverpod examples/pubspec.yaml:27-30
        sdk: flutter
      provider: ^6.0.0
-     flutter_riverpod: ^0.13.0


-     # The following adds the Cupertino Icons font to your application.
+     flutter_riverpod: ^0.14.0
+     # The following adds the Cupertino Icons font to your application.
      # Use with the CupertinoIcons class for iOS style icons.
      cupertino_icons: ^1.0.2

Accept change (y = yes, n = no [default], A = yes to all, q = quit)?
y
sanjib@sanjib-desktop:~/Documents/development/riverpod examples$ flutter run
Using hardware rendering with device Android SDK built for x86. If you notice graphic
rendering with "--enable-software-rendering".
Launching lib/main.dart on Android SDK built for x86 in debug mode...
Running Gradle task 'assembleDebug'...
```

Figure 19.2 – Riverpod migration taking place

As we have successfully migrated from the old version of Riverpod to the newest version, now we can run the Riverpod flutter app without any worry.

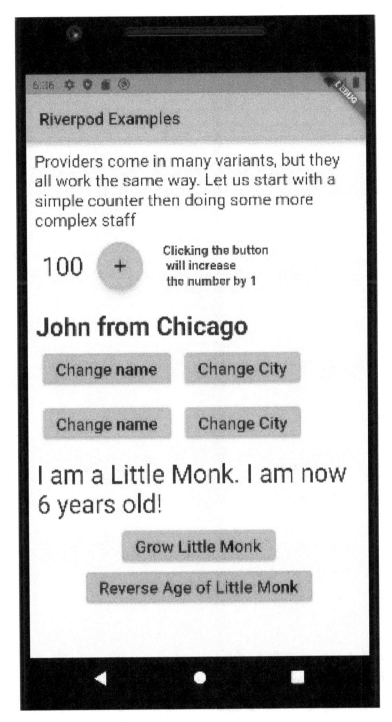

Figure 19.3 – Riverpod Flutter App after migration without any error

Incidentally, we don't have to change anything in our previous code. Certainly, we've only changed the theme primary swatch colour from blue to orange, so that we can differentiate between the old and the new.

Subsequently, we can click any button to change the provider value or you may say the state of the app.

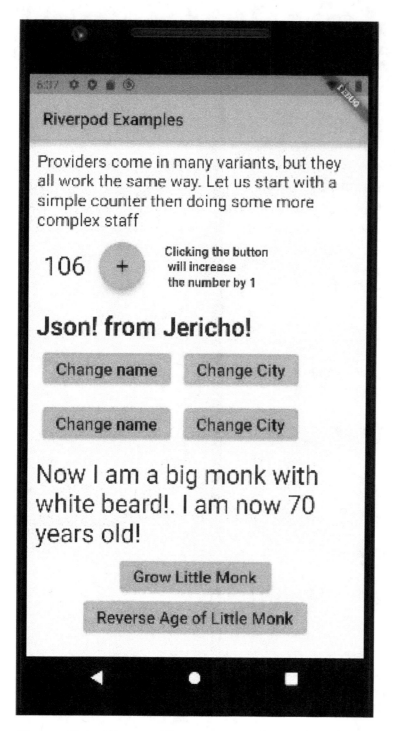

Figure 19.4 – Riverpod flutter app working after migration

Watch the change on the screen, and it works like a charm!

Why we need the latest Flutter and Dart SDK?

To use the latest Riverpod state management package we need to upgrade Flutter first. Therefore, for Riverpod latest version [0.14.0, or flutter_riverpod:]1.0.0-dev.11, our

Flutter SDK should also be the latest; that is Flutter 2.5.3 • channel stable • and a Dart SDK >= 2.14.0.

If we want to use the latest Riverpod first upgrade Flutter and Dart SDK. Otherwise, we get the error: Object.hash not found.

To be more precise, the error-output is quite long.

```
 1 ../../packages/riverpod/lib/src/common.dart:173:30: Error: Method
not found: 'Object\
 2 .hash'.
 3 int get hashCode => Object.hash(runtimeType, value);
 4                            ^^^^
 5 ../../packages/riverpod/lib/src/common.dart:374:30: Error: Method
not found: 'Object\
 6 .hash'.
 7 int get hashCode => Object.hash(runtimeType, previous);
 8                            ^^^^
 9 ../../packages/riverpod/lib/src/common.dart:415:30: Error: Method
not found: 'Object\
10 .hash'.
11 int get hashCode => Object.hash(runtimeType, error, stackTrace);
12                            ^^^^
13
14
15 FAILURE: Build failed with an exception.
16
17 * Where:
18 Script
'/home/nobu/snap/flutter/common/flutter/packages/flutter_tools/gradle/f
lutter\
19 .gradle' line: 1035
20
21 * What went wrong:
22 Execution failed for task ':app:compileFlutterBuildDebug'.
23 > Process 'command
'/home/nobu/snap/flutter/common/flutter/bin/flutter'' finished wi\
24 th non-zero exit value 1
25
26 * Try:
27 Run with --stacktrace option to get the stack trace. Run with --info
or --debug opti\
28 on to get more log output. Run with --scan to get full insights.
29
30 * Get more help at https://help.gradle.org
31
32 BUILD FAILED in 38s
33 Running Gradle task 'assembleDebug'...
34 Running Gradle task 'assembleDebug'... Done
```

```
42.4s
35 Exception: Gradle task assembleDebug failed with exit code 1
```

With reference to the above error, let us know a few important facts about hash code.

A hash code is a single integer which represents the state of the object. Not only that, it also affects operator == comparisons.

Now, each Object has unique identity, and the single integer hash code implements that. Now equality of two objects depends on default operator == implementation. Two objects are equal if and only if they are identical.

While using Riverpod state management, we must keep one thing in mind.

Why?

Because, it's an important concept. If the default operator == is overridden to use the object state the hash code must also be changed to represent that state.

Unequal objects may have the same hash code, but if it happens too often, clashes occur and the efficiency reduces affecting the data structures, such as HashSet or HashMap.

Is Riverpod better than Provider?

In the flutter community, many developers think Riverpod is better than Provider, which is an earlier-released-state-management package. However, flutter creators still recommend Provider as the stable state management mechanism at the time of writing this post.

According to the creator of both packages, Remi Rousselet, and other flutter developers as well, Provider has had some limitations. Riverpod has overcome those limitations.

Certainly, provider is a wrapper class or rather a kind of simplification of InheritedWidgets. On the contrary, Remi Rousselet has re-implemented InheritedWidget from the scratch and made Riverpod.

Both the state management packages have similarity and also has many differences.

As a state management package, provider has become enormously popular. Then why do we need another mechanism in place?

Provider can create, observe and dispose state without rebuilding widgets. It makes objects visible in Flutter's devtool. Testing and composing is not difficult. Since the data flow is unidirectional, the app is scalable.

These are all advantages that has made provider package so popular.

However, Riverpod has extended these benefits in a great way. It is compile-safe. It doesn't throw any run time exception. With riverpod we can have multiple providers of same type. It can make a provider private.

Above all, Riverpod is flutter independent as we can achieve the above mentioned features by not using InheritedWidgets any more. Riverpod implements its own mechanism.

What is new in Riverpod?

Firstly, we need to add the latest dependency.

```
1 dependencies:
2 flutter:
3     sdk: flutter
4 provider: ^6.0.0
5 flutter_riverpod: ^1.0.0-dev.11
```

Secondly, we can wrap our root with ProviderScope.

```
1 void main() {
2 runApp(
3     const ProviderScope(
4     child: ProviderAppSample(),
5     ),
6 }
```

From now on, all the providers we'll create, the ProviderScope will store the state of them.

The new concept in the latest Riverpod is the ref object of type WidgetRef.

What is a WidgetRef?

In the latest Riverpod, we can watch or read provider's value by using this ref object.

When we use Consumer or ConsumerState, the WidgetRef object is available as an argument, and it can interact with any provider.

As the BuildContext allows us to access the ancestor widgets in the widget tree, the WidgetRef does the same, allowing us to interact with any provider.

How does that happen?

Because all Riverpod providers are global so that we can access them easily. As a result, we can handle state management logic outside the widget tree.

We need to remember that Provider does not let us change the value. To do that we need to create a StateProvider. It will be a global value.

```
1 final referenceValue = StateProvider((ref) => 0);
```

Now, we can watch and read the provider's value quite easily.

```dart
1  import 'package:flutter/material.dart';
2
3  import 'package:flutter_riverpod/flutter_riverpod.dart';
4
5  class ProviderAppSample extends StatelessWidget {
6  const ProviderAppSample({Key? key}) : super(key: key);
7
8  @override
9  Widget build(BuildContext context) {
10     return const MaterialApp(
11     home: ProviderHome(),
12     );
13 }
14 }
15
16 final referenceValue = StateProvider((ref) => 0);
17
18 class ProviderHome extends ConsumerWidget {
19 const ProviderHome({Key? key}) : super(key: key);
20
21 @override
22 Widget build(BuildContext context, WidgetRef ref) {
23     final counterWatch = ref.watch(referenceValue);
24     final counterRead = ref.read(referenceValue);
25     return Scaffold(
26     body: Center(
27         child: Column(
28         children: [
29             Container(
30             margin: const EdgeInsets.all(20),
31             padding: const EdgeInsets.all(20),
32             child: Text(
33                 '${counterWatch.state}',
34                 style: const TextStyle(
35                 fontSize: 100,
36                 fontFamily: 'Allison',
37                 fontWeight: FontWeight.bold,
38                 color: Colors.red,
39                 ),
40             ),
41             ),
42             const SizedBox(
43             height: 20,
44             ),
45             ElevatedButton(
46             onPressed: () => counterRead.state++,
47             child: const Text(
48                 'Press to Increment',
```

```
49                    style: TextStyle(
50                    fontSize: 30,
51                    color: Colors.white,
52                    ),
53              ),
54              ),
55         ],
56         ),
57      ),
58      );
59 }
60 }
```

And we can access the provider's state quite easily.

```
1 Widget build(BuildContext context, WidgetRef ref) {
2     final counterWatch = ref.watch(referenceValue);
3     final counterRead = ref.read(referenceValue);
4 ...
```

And after that, we can either watch the change, and implement the change.

```
1 child: Text(
2                    '${counterWatch.state}',
3 ...
4 ElevatedButton(
5            onPressed: () => counterRead.state++,
6 ...
```

As a result, we can press the button and the number grows by 1.

Model class with StateNotifierProvider in new Riverpod

Before we learn how to use Riverpod StateNotifierProvider, let us know a few facts about state management in flutter.

To handle state management in a more systematic way in my website, we've created a separate category named "State Management" and that category has two sub-categories named "Riverpod" and "Provider".

Therefore you may read the updated flutter articles there. For more Flutter related Articles and Resources

Although we've started with Riverpod StateNotifierProvider, the next article will be on a gentle introduction on state management itself. And after that, we'll delve into Provider and Riverpod state management package simultaneously, so that a beginner can understand the core concepts behind these beautiful state management system.

Usually for simple counter we don't need Riverpod StateNotifierProvider. It helps us to manage more complex data model. However, let's use a simple use case like a counter app that changes its state and the number increases as the user presses the button below.

With reference to either Provider or Riverpod package, we can run the below code sample firstly. Secondly, we'll discuss code.

The above counter displays a number 0. From where that number has come, we'll see in our code in a minute.

Now, as we press the floating action button below, the state of the app changes and we get the next number 1.

Broadly speaking, it's a very simple app and usually comes by default when we create a flutter app. However, that's a stateful widget that manages state of the app automatically.

To tell the truth, we don't have any stateful widget in place. But we're managing state with the help of Riverpod package.

We have to add the dependency first in our pubspec.yaml file.

```
1 dependencies:
2 flutter:
3      sdk: flutter
4 provider: ^6.0.0
5 flutter_riverpod: ^1.0.0-dev.11
```

Then we have a simple counter data model class like the following one.

```
1 import 'package:flutter_riverpod/flutter_riverpod.dart';
2
3 class Countering extends StateNotifier<int> {
4 Countering() : super(0);
5
6 void increment() => state++;
7 }
```

The above class sets the initial state in the constructor.

```
1 Countering() : super(0);
```

The number 0 in the above screenshot comes from the initial state that we've mentioned in the constructor.

Next, we can create a new provider like the following.

```
1 final counterProvider =
2      StateNotifierProvider<Countering, int>((ref) => Countering());
```

Now, we can use the following code to get the state of the app.

```
1 final counter = ref.watch(counterProvider);
```

And, to change the state we use read method.

```
1 onPressed: () {
2         ref.read(counterProvider.notifier).increment();
3         },
```

In the Countering model, we have used StateNotifier as an extension that acts as the place where our business logic goes. The Riverpod service reads and writes using Countering model that extends StateNotifier and talks to the relevant widgets.

Let's see the full code.

```
1 import 'package:flutter/material.dart';
2 import 'package:flutter_artisan/models/countering.dart';
3 import 'package:flutter_riverpod/flutter_riverpod.dart';
4
5 class StateNotifierProviderAppSample extends StatelessWidget {
6 const StateNotifierProviderAppSample({Key? key}) : super(key: key);
7
8 @override
9 Widget build(BuildContext context) {
10     return const MaterialApp(
11     home: StateNotifierProviderHome(),
12     );
13 }
14 }
15
16 final counterProvider =
17     StateNotifierProvider<Countering, int>((ref) => Countering());
18
19 class StateNotifierProviderHome extends ConsumerWidget {
20 const StateNotifierProviderHome({Key? key}) : super(key: key);
21
22 @override
23 Widget build(BuildContext context, WidgetRef ref) {
24     final counter = ref.watch(counterProvider);
25     return Scaffold(
26     body: Center(
27         child: Container(
28         margin: const EdgeInsets.all(20),
29         padding: const EdgeInsets.all(20),
30         child: Text(
31             '$counter',
32             style: const TextStyle(
33             fontSize: 60,
34             color: Colors.red,
35             ),
36         ),
37         ),
38         ),
```

```
39      floatingActionButton: FloatingActionButton(
40          backgroundColor: Colors.deepOrange,
41          tooltip: 'Press to Increment',
42          onPressed: () {
43          ref.read(counterProvider.notifier).increment();
44          },
45          child: const Icon(Icons.add),
46      ),
47      );
48 }
49 }
```

Most importantly we have used ProviderScope so every child gets the service properly.

```
1 void main() {
2 runApp(
3      const ProviderScope(
4      child: StateNotifierProviderAppSample(),
5      ),
6 }
```

From onward we'll get updated articles on State Management in my website, so feel free to read those articles and if you want to know anything, please drop a line in the comment section.

For more Flutter related Articles and Resources

20. What Next

I hope this book on state management in Flutter helps you to choose the right option that you're searching.

Every Flutter Application is different, but you can solve most state management riddles with any single Provider variant of Riverpod package.

I have used more than one code repositories for this book.

You will get the links below.

The first code repository for this book

The second code repository for this book

The third code repository for this book

The fourth code repository for this book

For more Flutter related Articles and Resources